ALL-AMERICAN FRANK:

A HISTORY OF THE HOT DOG

by Robert W. Bly

PublishAmerica
Baltimore

First printing

ISBN: 1-4137-5062-1

PUBLISHED BY PUBLISHAMERICA, LLLP

www.publishamerica.com

Baltimore

Printed in the United States of America

Cook: Today's special is franks and beans.

Dagwood: No, not today.

Cook: I thought you liked hot dogs.

Dagwood: I do. But I had two of 'em on my way over here.

—From a *Blondie* cartoon strip, *New York Daily News*, February 18, 1999

It (the hot dog) represents a predictability of life; everything changes, but the hot dog remains the same. It's a comfort food that crosses all socioeconomic levels. It's like returning home.

– Gloria Pink, owner, Pink's hot dog stand

PREFACE

If ketchup, as Andrew Smith claims in his book *Pure Ketchup*, is "America's national condiment," then hot dogs are surely America's national food.

Hot dogs—also known as franks, frankfurters, or wieners—were ranked as America's third-favorite food in 1994 behind pizza (#1) and sandwiches (#2). If you were to place all the hot dogs consumed in the U.S. each year end to end, they'd reach to the moon and back three times.

Every year, Americans eat about 20 billion hot dogs. Between Memorial Day and Labor Day alone this year, Americans will eat 7 billion hot dogs, reports Oscar Mayer. If these hot dogs were laid end to end, they would form a link of dogs 500 times longer than the distance between California and New York.

According to the National Hot Dog and Sausage Council, 95 percent of Americans serve hot dogs in their homes. The average American eats 80 hot dogs a year.

Hot dogs are a staple of American culinary culture from backyard barbecues to ball games. Like Dr. Seuss's green eggs and ham, people will eat hot dogs anywhere—and they can, since hot dogs are a uniquely portable food: meat in a tube with a casing and roll to prevent spillage, mess, and burned hands. "It has been said that the most loyal and most noble dog of all is the hot dog," comments Burt Wolf, a New York food writer and restaurateur. "It feeds the hand that bites it."

While hot dogs are not health food, they are in fact healthier and less fattening than many other popular foods. A hot dog on a bun has only 260 calories, compared with 370 calories in a peanut butter and jelly sandwich and 440 calories in a cheeseburger. That same hot dog contains 15 grams of fat vs. 26 grams for a breaded fish sandwich on a roll with tartar sauce (the new low-fat hot dogs have one to two grams of fat each). Hot dogs were included on the NASA-approved menus for the Skylab and Apollo space missions. A recent hot dog innovation is a wiener casing made of cellulose, which allows franks to have ads and other promotional messages imprinted on them.

In *All-American Frank: A History of the Hot Dog,* you get the inside story of the history, manufacture, marketing, cooking, selling, and consumption of frankfurters. It's a frank (pun intended) appraisal of the hot dog's many roles in nutrition, cuisine, the food industry, and American popular culture.

The book covers the history, development, and rising popularity of the hot dog. It presents recipes, both for making your own hot dogs and using store-bought franks as a cooking ingredient. It also covers the different manufacturers and brands, and provides ordering information for those brands sold by mail.

When I told a friend I was doing this book, he asked, "Why on Earth would anyone write—or read—a book about hot dogs?"

I suppose I could have quoted Daphne Derven, director of the American Center for Wine, Food and the Arts, who said, "Throughout human history, people have paid attention to what they eat. Food is a necessity, but also something we choose to devote an extraordinary amount of care and thought to. It's part of who we are."

Instead, I told him that I just like hot dogs. If you do too, enjoy this book… and your next dog!

I do have a favor to ask. If you have a great hot dog story or recipe, why not send it to me so we can share it with readers of the next edition of this book? You will receive full credit, of course.

Bob Bly
22 E. Quackenbush Avenue
Dumont, NJ 07628
phone 201-385-1220
fax 201-385-1138
e-mail: rwbly@bly.com
Web site: www.bly.com

Table of Contents

Chapter 1:

Hot Dog Roots

When you think about it, a hot dog is an extremely weird way to eat a piece of cow.

You take the cow. Chop it up. Stuff it into a tube. Put the meat-stuffed tube into an elongated bun. Then cover it with mustard—a condiment you'd never use on a steak.

I know that's a gross description. But of course, it's absolutely true.

Hot dogs taste great. But it's a little crazy. Why not just slice the meat from the cow and cook it? If you find it easier to eat chopped meat, then by all means chop it, but why shove it into a tube?

(Jim Rockford, the detective played by James Garner on the TV show *The Rockford Files,* referred to hot dogs as "tube steaks." He grilled them frequently on his charcoal barbecue because he was usually flat broke and could not afford filet mignon or a T-bone.)

Who came up with this? How? And why? When exploring the history of hot dogs, keep in mind that consumers usually desire the following characteristics in their food:

- The dish is tasty. People prefer spicy to bland.

- Health has traditionally been of secondary importance to taste. People want good nutrition, but given a nutritious snack and a tasty one, they often grab the food that tastes best.

- Convenience is a big factor. Is the food easy to get, to prepare, and to eat? Can it be prepared rapidly? The fact that "fast food" is a multi-billion dollar industry today is not accidental.

- Cost is also a factor. Traditionally the largest percentage of the world's wealth is concentrated within a small segment of the population. This means most people are on a budget and are looking to eat cheap.

- Finally, there's the fun factor. People like to eat foods that are "fun"—hot dogs, popcorn, cotton candy. Kellogg's made a best-seller of Rice Krispies based on the seemingly inconsequential fact that it made noise in the bowl (remember snap, crackle, pop?). Cheez Whiz caught on because it is cheese that sprays out of a can. Cracker Jack became the #1 brand of caramel-coated popcorn because of the cheap prize inside every box. Ball Park Franks are advertised as hot dogs that grow in size before your eyes while you prepare them (they "plump when you cook 'em").

Market research conducted by The Consumer Network shows that consumers have definite preferences when buying packaged meats in the supermarket; hot dogs seem to satisfy most of these requirements too:

1. Easy to store. Hot dogs come neatly packaged with individual servings (the hot dogs) already separated vs. a package of chopped meat which must be pressed into

hamburger patties by hand. More and more supermarkets are offering, at a higher price per pound than regular chopped meat, chopped meat already pressed into hamburger patties.

2. Oven friendly. "Meat that can be popped right into any kind of oven in its packaging saves both preparation and clean-up time," one study reports. Hot dogs must be removed from their plastic wrapper for cooking, but the individual hot dogs are packaged in their casings, making them easy to handle and heat.

3. See through. Consumers prefer packaging through which the meat can be seen, and of course, this is how hot dogs are packaged. They also like packages with large, easy-to-read labels that don't fade in the refrigerator and freezer, and virtually all major hot dog brands comply.

4. Nutrition-friendly. Consumers want to know that the nutritional value isn't going to leach or fade through the package during storage. Hot dogs are sealed in air-tight plastic which stays clean and dry on the outside—another important consumer preference when buying meat.

5. Easily opened. Hot dogs do only so-so here. Often the tight plastic packaging is tough to remove without a knife or scissors, and when you open it, juice spills out.

A Brief History of the Sausage

Frankfurters, along with bologna, salami, and kielbasa, are technically a type of sausage. A "sausage" is any meat stuffed into a casing and cooked or cured.

Cooking, of course, means to heat the meat. Most of the meat we eat is cooked, but not all. Steak tartar, for example, was once a popular restaurant dish, made by mixing raw ground beef with a raw egg, salt, and other spices.

Steak tartar has declined in popularity, and you don't see it served much anymore. The main reason is probably the increasing incidence of beef contaminated by bacteria, which makes uncooked meat unsafe to eat. However, reports of contaminated raw fish have also become more frequent, yet people still eat sushi—raw fish wrapped in rice and seaweed—with abandon. (One chef jokingly refers to steak tartar as "cow sushi.")

Nutritionists believe fish is good for your heart, and red meat isn't. That may be the reason why sushi thrives while steak tartar has faded.

About half of the sausage made is cooked, but half isn't. The uncooked half isn't raw, strictly speaking. It's cured.

There are two major types of sausage: wet and dry. Dry sausages are cured. Wet are cooked.

Dry sausages typically have little moisture, do not need to be refrigerated, and can be eaten right out of the package—no heating required. Salami is a dry sausage, as are pepperoni, summer sausage, and Slim Jims. Dry sausages are usually eaten cold, either as sticks of meat (Slim Jims), slices, toppings (pepperoni on pizza), or in sandwiches. Beef jerky, a dried meat steak sold at convenience store counters, is a popular dried sausage.

Dry sausages are also used as an ingredient in other dishes. In 1997, Hebrew National, the hot dog maker, held its first salami cook-off in Manhattan to promote salami sales. The winning dish? Salami Napoleon. Its creator, Eli Brown, used thin layers of crisply fried potatoes with onions, tomatoes, and spinach sautéed in olive oil, alternating with layers of fried salami. The dish was garnished with sautéed tomatoes, onions, spinach, and sour cream.

Non-dairy sour cream was used to enable the dish to comply with kosher dietary laws, which do not allow meat and milk to be eaten together. (Jewish law strives to make people less cruel. The ethical principle behind this particular dietary restriction of not eating meat and milk together is that it is cruel to boil the calf in the milk of its mother.)

I grew up in a Jewish household in the 1960s. Both salami and hot dogs were staples of our diet, and I loved each. Since dried sausage tastes good cold, and wet sausages—such as hot dogs—don't, I carried a salami sandwich on rye with mustard in my lunch bag to high school daily. In 1964, my family brown-bagged salami sandwiches to the World's Fair, so we would not have to buy food from what my father viewed as overpriced concessionaires.

Wet sausages, by comparison, are often juicy, must be refrigerated, and should be cooked before consuming. Two examples of wet sausage are the breakfast links you have with your eggs in the morning, and the Italian or Polish sausage you eat on rolls with onions and peppers at carnivals and street fairs. Hot dogs are also a wet sausage; in fact, the average hot dog is ten percent water.

The dry sausages are, for the most part, cured meats. Curing is a process that transforms meat into a physical form digestible and safe to eat, without the heat of cooking, usually by chemical means.

"Cure" is the mixture of ingredients blended into the ground or chopped meat that causes this chemical change to take place. Ingredients used in cures include salt, sugar, sodium nitrate, sodium nitrite, and potassium nitrate. The cure is mixed in with the dry meat, and the mixture sits for a period of time as the curing takes place.

Hot dogs, as wet sausages, are not cured. They are smoked or cooked—usually cooked.

What is smoked food? And how is it different from cured food? Chemicals in smoke—aldehydes, phenols, ketones, and carbolic acid—are absorbed by the food, preserving the meat and adding flavor.

The preservative power of smoke has long been known. Thousands of years ago in Peru, for example, mummies were made by removing the soft parts of the body, then drying the body with heat and curing it with smoke.

Smoking and salting were the first techniques developed for meat preservation. The process kills certain microbes that cannot live in a salty environment. Spices can also make preserved meat easier to digest and even cover up the bad taste of partially spoiled meat. Americans love spicing their food; the average American uses 3.7 pounds of spices per year.

Because of its value in preserving and seasoning meat, spice became a precious commodity among civilized societies during the Middle Ages. Brought to western and northern Europe, spices were shipped to England, Ireland, France, and the Netherlands.

The Hanseatic merchants traded spices in the North Sea and the Baltic areas. Northern Italian and southern German merchants bought and sold spices overland and via the Alps. Venice, Genoa, Lisbon, London, Dublin, Amsterdam, Lubeck, and other harbor towns became wealthy because of the spice trade. So did inland towns such as Constance, Augsburg, Nuremberg, and Krakow.

The use of spice, particularly pepper, came to be regarded as a status symbol. Duke Karl of Bourgogne, one of the wealthiest men in Europe, ordered 380 pounds of pepper for his wedding dinner in 1468. No mention is made in the history books of whether sausage was on the menu, or whether the couple sneezed during their vows.

Sausage Invented B.C.

Sausage was made by the Babylonians more than 3,500 years ago by stuffing spiced meat into animal intestines. It may have been eaten even earlier; sausage was mentioned as far back as the 9th century B.C. in Homer's *Odyssey*.

Greeks considered sausage a delicacy high up on the scale of culinary arts. The Greek author Ephicharmus wrote a play entitled *Orya*, which translates into "The Sausage." And in a play written by Aristophanes around 423 B.C., a character says "Let them make sausage of me and serve me up to the students." Sausage is mentioned in one of the earliest cookbooks, written by Athenaeus in 228 A.D.

Constantine the Great, Emperor of Rome, banned the populace from eating sausage, feeling that it should be restricted to the banquet tables of royalty. Ironically, today the hot dog is viewed as anything but a gourmet item. People from all walks of life love and eat them. Indeed, the low price and easy preparation have made them a traditional family meal favorite. Finer restaurants, by contrast, do not serve them; you never see a hot dog on a dinner menu next to the filet mignon or beef Wellington, except perhaps on the children's menu.

(Ironically, Bill Handwerker, grandson of Nathan Handwerker, founder of the famous Coney Island hot dog restaurant, recently announced his plans to help launch a new chain of theme restaurants that *won't* be serving hot dogs; they'll feature steaks instead.)

The Roman commoners continued to make sausage at home in secret, lest they be caught and punished. Eventually the Roman sausage ban was repealed.

The word sausage is derived from the Latin word *salsus*, meaning salted or preserved. The Greek word for sausage is *oryae*. Sausage was a popular dish with the Babylonians, some 1,500 years ago. Fifth-century B.C. literature refers to salami, a type of sausage thought to have originated on the east coast of Cyprus.

In the United States, there are approximately 2,100 meat processors producing 5.2 billion pounds of over 200 different sausages annually. Nineteen billion of these sausages are hot dogs.

Today two types of casings are used: animal and plant. The animal casings, as in ancient Greece, are made from the cleaned and salted intestines of animals—usually those from which the filling was taken. The plant casings are made from cellulose, a material composed of plant tissues and fibers. Some sausages, such as breakfast patties, are made without casings.

Cellulose, like paper, is made primarily of fiber, and like paper, cellulose can be written on. In 1990, Viskase Corporation of Chicago developed a casing, the E-Z Mark Nojax, on which advertising messages could be imprinted to appear on the hot dogs.

Many types of sausages were named after the city in which they were first made. Frankfurters, for instance, were first made in Frankfurt, Germany. Genoa salami originated in Genoa, Italy; bologna was invented in Bologna, Italy.

The ancient Greek sausages were somewhat plain and usually unspiced. It wasn't until the Middle Ages that people began adding spices to the meat. Salami and pepperoni are two of the most highly seasoned sausages.

Nineteenth-century cookbook author Marion Harland gave the following recipe for home-made sausage:

6 lbs. lean fresh pork
3 lbs. fat fresh pork
12 teaspoonfuls powdered sage
6 teaspoonfuls black pepper
6 teaspoonfuls salt
2 teaspoonfuls powdered mace
2 teaspoonfuls powdered cloves
1 grated nutmeg

Grind the meat, fat and lean, in a sausage-mill, or chop it very fine. The mill is better, and grinding does not occupy one-tenth of the time that chopping does, to say nothing of the labor. One can be bought for three or four dollars, and will well repay the purchaser. Mix the seasoning in with your hands, taste to be sure all is right, and pack down in stone jars, pouring melted lard on top. Another good way of preserving them is to make long, narrow bags of stout muslin, large enough to contain, each, enough sausage for a family dish. Fill these with the meat, dip in melted lard, and hang from the beams of the cellar.

If you wish to pack in the intestines of the hog, they should be carefully prepared as follows: Empty them, cut them in lengths, and lay them for two days in salt and water. Turn them inside out, and lay in soak one day longer. Scrape them, rinse well in soda and water, wipe, and blow into one end, having tied up the other with a bit of twine. If they are whole and clear, stuff with the meat; tie up and hang in the store-room or cellar.

These are fried in the cases, in a clean, dry frying-pan, until brown. If you have sausage-meat in bulk, make into small, round flat cakes, and fry in the same way. Some dip in egg and pounded cracker-others roll in flour before cooking. Their own fat will cook them. Send to table dry and hot, but do not let them fry hard. When one side is done, turn to the other. The fire should be very brisk. Ten minutes, or twelve at the outside, is long enough to cook them.

Hot Dog Origins

In *The New Hamburger & Hot Dog Cookbook*, Mettja C. Roate discusses possible origins of today's modern hot dog:

> Who invented the wiener or hot dog as we know it today is open to claim and debate. One school of thought maintains that it was invented in the 1850s by an enterprising Austrian. He named his sausage "Wien" after Vienna, Austria.
>
> There is another school of thought which maintains that the hot dog was invented by an ambitious butcher in Frankfurt on Main in Germany at about the same time. He called his tasty sausages "frankfurters."

Other histories claim an earlier origin for the frank. An article on the Web site of the National Hot Dog & Sausage Council (www.hot-dog.org) says the frankfurter was invented in Frankfurt not in the 1850s, but in 1484—eight years before Columbus set sail for the new world.

Another possible city of origin is Coburg, Germany, where—in the late 1600s—Johann Georghehner, a butcher, created a popular sausage known as the "dachshund" or "little-dog" sausage because of its dachshund-like shape. As you will read in chapter 2, the dog shape of the sausage led to the name hot dog when it was brought to the United States.

It cannot be precisely determined whether the American hot dog was adapted from the German frankfurter, the Austrian wiener, or the Czech parkys, all of which share a common heritage.

Roate continues:

> Where the wiener really made its big mark was at Coney Island in New York.
>
> The gentleman who put the hot dog into the everyday vocabulary was Nathan Handwerker [when] he started his very first Nathan's Famous Coney Island Hot Dog Stand.

To promote sales of his hot dogs, Handwerker hired wholesome-looking young men to hang around his hot dog carts and eat hot dogs in full view of people strolling the boardwalk. He dressed the young men in starched white coats to give the impression that they were doctors or interns (legend has it that he even had them carry stethoscopes in their pockets). Visitors to Coney Island figured that if the hot dogs, which only cost a nickel at the time, were being eaten by doctors, they had to be healthy.

While Nathan's is the most famous Coney Island hot dog stand (the word "famous" being part of the actual name of the stand), it was not the first. That honor belongs to the Coney Island hot dog stand opened by Charles Feltman, a German immigrant, in 1871. His first year in business, Feltman sold 3,684 hot dogs. By 1901, Feltman's business had grown from a hot dog cart to a huge Coney Island restaurant, "Feltman's German Gardens."

Nathan Handwerker, founder of Nathan's Famous, began his career in the hot dog business in 1914 working at Feltman's restaurant. According to stories passed down by the Handwerker family, Nathan was at the serving counter of Feltman's. Two of his friends—singing waiter Eddie Cantor and piano player Jimmy Durante (then at the beginning of their own careers and virtually unknown)—complained to him that ten cents was a lot of money to pay for a hot dog.

This gave Nathan the idea of opening a competing stand that sold hot dogs at a nickel apiece. So he scraped together $300, and in the spring of 1916, at the corner of Surf and Stillwell Avenues, he opened up his own stand and started selling hot dogs for five cents, a price that included a root beer and a pickle. If the root beer was worth a penny and the pickle another penny, Nathan's was essentially selling the hot dog for three cents, undercutting Feltman's price by a hefty 70 percent.

Nathan had been a shoemaker once, back in Belgium, to which he had moved from his birthplace, Galicia, in Eastern Europe. In 1912, at age 20, along with tens of thousands of other immigrants, he arrived in New York City.

Finding that there was no shortage of shoemakers in New York, Nathan took a position as dishwasher and counterman at a lower Manhattan restaurant called Max's Busy Bee. Weekends he moonlighted at Feltman's German Gardens out on Coney Island.

Shortly after he opened his stand, Handwerker hired a smart young woman named Ida Greenwald to come to work for him, and then married her. He credited Ida with being the real brains behind the operation, starting with the "secret special sauce" that distinguished Nathan's original red hots.

At first the stand simply had an oil cloth sign that said "Hot Dogs." When a customer complained that the restaurant was hard to find, Nathan pointed out the sign. "Yes, but you don't say whose hot dogs. Your stand needs a name," she replied.

Handwerker thought about calling the business Handwerker's Hot Dogs, perhaps because he liked the alliteration. But at the time, a song called "Nathan, Nathan, Why You Waiting?"

became popular. Handwerker decided that because Nathan was his real first name and the song was promoting the name, he would call his place simply "Nathan's." He added the "Famous" later.

In 1923, the New York subway system was extended to Coney Island, and enormous crowds began spilling out of the Stillwell Avenue station. Many of them headed straight to Nathan's, and Nathan's stayed open 24 hours a day.

Broadway and Hollywood stars, gangsters, VIPs, socialites, and politicians were among the clientele at Nathan's. Nelson Rockefeller once commented, "No one can hope to be elected in this state without being photographed eating a hot dog at Nathan's Famous."

Customers ate standing up and wiped their mouths with napkins. In 1936, when President Franklin Roosevelt entertained King George VI and Queen Elizabeth of England at Hyde Park, he fed them Nathan's hot dogs. The first lady, Eleanor Roosevelt, was a fan of Nathan's hot dogs and helped make them popular. In the early1940s, Nathan's stand at Surf and Stillwell launched an annual hot dog eating contest that fast became firmly installed in the American culture, regularly celebrated in the newsreels.

By late 1954, Nathan Handwerker was selling 6 million dogs a year and his son Murray was president of the Coney Island Chamber of Commerce. They were staunch Coney Island preservationists who fought Robert Moses' plan to rebuild or rearrange everything in New York City. The dogs themselves had gone up in price to 25 cents. But they still were eight-inch dogs. "Moses has shrunk the amusement center of Coney Island considerably," Nathan said on one public occasion. "But never, and I mean never, will he shrink Nathan's frankfurters."

Nathan's had become a big business now, and Murray regularly urged his father to think about expanding beyond Surf and Stillwell. "What for?" He always shrugged, gazing out at the beach and the boardwalk and the sun and the sea. "I got everything I need right here."

Murray didn't share his father's view. In 1962, the old family business started opening other locations—in Oceanside, L.I., in Yonkers, in Times Square, elsewhere. In 1968, the company went public. Within just a couple of years, the shareholders were complaining about management. Nathan's dogs were 40 cents now. That was hard to believe, but Nathan was philosophical in his old age. "If hot dogs were still selling for five cents," he mused in August 1970, "the country would be in bad shape."

Nathan's continued to be a favorite among the jet set. Barbara Streisand had Nathan's cater the closing-night party for *Funny Girl* in London. The hot dogs were flown in from 3,000 miles away. Customers included motion picture industry heavyweights such as Jack Warner, Alan Arkin, Maximillian Schell, George Segal, and Robert Goulet, many of whom had Nathan's served on location when shooting films.

Nathan Handwerker died in Florida at 83 on March 25, 1974, spared the heartbreak of having to watch his legendary Nathan's Famous fall apart. At the time of his death, the company was deep into franchising and there were several dozen Nathan's Famous locations in the city and its environs.

Many of them were poorly run; one of them in particular, at Eighth St. and Sixth Ave. in Manhattan, became the target of a Greenwich Village activist crusade in the late 1970s as it turned into a shooting gallery given wide berth by neighborhood residents. It was finally thrown off the block, and in the early 1980s the increasingly hard-pressed chain shut down 20 more of its metro stores.

In December 1986, Nathan's Famous was sold off to a syndicate of investors for $17 million. The more or less original

Nathan's still stands at Surf and Stillwell on Coney Island, just where its founder built it.

Today many hot dog aficionados still consider the Nathan's frank to be one of the better hot dogs. In the 2000s, many fast food vendors began seeking economy of scale by having two or more franchises in a single location. Therefore you can find an Arthur Treacher's and a Kentucky Fried Chicken sharing a single restaurant. In the same way, Blimpie's subs and Nathan's now coexist at one location near my office, as do Baskin-Robbins and Dunkin' Donuts.

Another familiar New York City landmark is Nedick's, a chain of small restaurants, usually positioned on a busy street corner, where the favorite meal is a Shofar hot dog on a butter-toasted split-top roll, with orange drink as the preferred beverage. Other popular beverages consumed with a Nedick's hot dog are root beer and egg creams, another New York tradition.

An egg cream is a chocolate soda drink containing neither eggs nor cream. To make an egg cream, pour chocolate syrup in a large glass—the same amount as if you were mixing chocolate milk. Next, fill close to the top with seltzer or club soda. Stir gently; if you stir too vigorously, the drink will foam up and overflow the glass. Now top off with whole milk and stir.

In addition to the standard Shofar hot dog, Nedick's also offers Texas corn dogs, a Wisconsin brat, a Cincinnati Coney with chili, a Georgia fire dog, a California dog with guacamole, and a New Jersey ripper, which is deep fried.

Nedick's opened in 1913 and lasted through the 1970s, during which it closed its doors. In 2003, The Riese Organization, which also owns Nathan's, bought the Nedick's name and opened a Nedick's again in Manhattan, with plans for many future locations in the works.

The Hot Dog Today

Nathan made his original hot dogs from beef. Today hot dogs are made from beef, pork, veal, chicken, or turkey. Some have casings, and some do not. A hot dog usually contains 30 percent fat. Hot dog lovers, a group to which I proudly belong, by and large prefer hot dogs made from beef, and we look for "beef" or "all beef" on the label. Products labeled so must, by law, contain only beef—no soybean protein, dry milk solids, or other fillers are permitted.

"Kosher" added to the label of an "all-beef" frank means the hot dog is 100 percent cow. If the hot dog is labeled "all beef" but not kosher, it may contain pork as well as beef—typically 40 percent pork and 60 percent beef.

On the other hand, if the product is simply labeled "frankfurter," with no reference to beef or all-beef, they can contain fillers as well as chicken or turkey. Most franks contain sodium nitrite and sodium nitrate, two chemical salts many consumers prefer not to ingest (see chapter 5 for details).

Hot dogs can range in size from tiny cocktail franks to the popular "foot long" 12-inch giants. Most restaurants and stands sell hot dogs approximately six inches in length. Sara Lee once made a 1,996-foot hot dog—the longest ever created—to celebrate the 1996 Olympics.

"A good hot dog is all beef, and not pumped up with fillers which shrivel over the heat of the grill," comments Mark Di Ionno, a staff reporter for the *New Jersey Star Ledger.* "A great hot dog doesn't overpower the palate, but has enough flavor to hold its own against mustard, chili sauce, chopped onions, relish, ketchup—or some or all of the above." Packaged hot dogs, notes Di Ionno, usually come five or six to a pound.

What does a hot dog lover look for in the perfect dog?

- *Beef.* Beef is the preferred dog. Turkey and chicken are considered "diet dogs" and lack the true hot dog taste. The purer and better the quality of the meat, the better the hot dog—which is why so many hot dog lovers prefer kosher dogs.
- *Texture.* The casing should be slightly crisp and have a "snap" when you bite into it. Piercing the casing with your teeth should release some of the hot, flavorful juice within the dog's interior into your mouth and onto your taste buds. The inside should be firm, not mushy, and slightly chewy.
- *Spice.* The word that comes to mind when discussing a good hot dog is "savory." Aside from the content—meat and filler—the other variable between hot dog brands is the spicing. The spice should complement the flavor of the meat, rather than serve as a substitute for it.
- *Bun.* The purist demands a white bread bun—no hard roll, potato roll, or whatever roll. No Italian bread or hero roll. On occasion, when craving a hot dog but out of buns, I have eaten my frank folded up in a piece of fresh delicatessen rye bread, and found it a most pleasing repast. The rye has to be ultra-fresh, or it will break in half when folded, making the dog hard to hold. Another popular sandwich, the lobster roll, is made by putting fresh lobster salad in a hot dog roll.
- *Toppings.* The variety of toppings is discussed in chapter 7, and even the purists debate what is best. No topping and mustard-only are top choices, followed by relish, onions, and chili. Kids often prefer ketchup. Anyone putting mayonnaise on a hot dog should immediately seek psychiatric counseling.

Although brands vary, the basic formula for the hot dog has not changed at all since Nathan's first popularized hot dogs at its Coney Island restaurant. The main "advancement" is in distribution—the widespread popularity of the hot dog, and where it is served. This we discuss in the next chapter.

Chapter 2:

The Ubiquitous Hot Dog

The modern frankfurter is a variation of "dachshund sausage," a smoked, thin sausage developed in Germany in the 1850s and eaten with mustard and sauerkraut. This chapter examines how this one-time novelty snack became one of the most popular and endearing American foods. You've no doubt heard the expression "As American as hot dogs and apple pie." What makes a European invention so distinctly beloved in the U.S.A.?

One reason for their current popularity is that minimal preparation is required to eat hot dogs as a meal. You simply heat and serve. This quick preparation suits the lifestyle of today's busy families.

A *Parade* magazine survey revealed that more than half of Americans want a dinner they can prepare in only 15 to 30 minutes. Hot dogs take a few minutes in the broiler or on the grill, and only a minute or so in the microwave. In fact, supermarket sales of ready-to-heat meals are now $44 billion annually.

As mentioned in chapter 1, hot dogs are actually pre-cooked, so you can eat them raw, although few people do so. Raw hot dogs were a favorite snack of the late Walt Disney; his maid would serve them to him unheated right out of the refrigerator.

Interestingly, Disney rewarded her loyal service with frequent gifts of Disney stock; her Christmas present would also be Disney stock. With the profits from these stocks, she would simply buy more stock.

She didn't know much about the stock market, but she knew she worked for a smart, successful man, so she kept all the Disney stock Walt gave her over the years, and kept his refrigerator well-stocked with hot dogs. She also used every spare penny she had to acquire more Disney stock. At the time of her death, Disney's maid had an estate worth $9 million, which she left to her disabled son.

Another reason hot dogs are so popular is the low cost. The original hot dogs at Nathan's on Coney Island sold for a nickel apiece in 1916. Today, on the streets of New York City, you can get a kosher frank on a roll for only $1.50. This is the same city where my wife and I recently paid over $4 for an iced coffee drink at one of Manhattan's pricey and upscale coffee shops.

At a recent fair in our town, sausage and pepper sandwiches were $5 apiece. I feasted on a hot dog from the same grill, smothered in the same peppers, for only $1.50.

In Passaic, New Jersey, a Boy Scout troop recently replaced steak with hot dogs at their fundraising dinners. The reason: with rising prices, serving steak forced them to charge $30 or $35 per plate. By switching to hot dogs, they were able to sell plates for only $10 each.

Americans eat about 20 billion hot dogs annually—7 billion between Memorial Day and Labor Day, with 150 million of these consumed on the Fourth of July weekend alone. "Hot dogs are no doubt as poisonous as everyone says," writes Barbara Holland, "but on this special day nothing replaces their combination of textures—the squish of the bun, followed by the rubbery resistance of the hot dog's skin, followed by its familiar meaty interior and classic childhood flavor." Because of the surge in hot dog consumption on the Fourth of July in particular and the summer in general, July has been designated National Hot Dog Month by the United States Chamber of Commerce.

In a recent survey, almost one out of three parents polled said their children requested hot dogs at picnics and barbecues more than any other food. Hamburgers, with 27 percent, were the second choice.

Eighty-four percent of these parents said they served hot dogs within the past year. Fifty percent gave ease of preparation as the reason for cooking dogs, and 34 percent said they grilled franks because the kids liked them so much.

Because of this, hot dogs are sometimes thought of as a children's food, not an adult meal. At a recent Bar Mitzvah, the adults were served their choice of salmon, beef, or chicken, all smothered by some fancy sauce. A separate kids' table contained none of these dishes, and was instead laden with foods kids presumably like, chief among them, hot dogs. One of the other dads sitting at my table saw me looking at the hot dogs; a minute later, we both made a beeline for the kid's table. The two franks I ate, to me, were far superior to the adult fare.

Hot dogs are definitely a family food and a food for the young. Large families with five or more members, as well as younger families where the parents are under 35, eat more hot dogs than other consumers. Southerners eat more hot dogs than do people in other parts of the country. Young children often prefer their hot dog "naked" (without a roll), either whole or cut up on a plate.

In 1987, the last year for which the U.S. Department of Agriculture kept track of processed meat sales, the USDA reported the production of 1.5 billion pounds of meat franks and wieners. That's heavier than six oil tankers combined!

The National Hot Dog and Sausage Council estimates that annual hot dog production is approximately 2 billion pounds. This breaks down as follows:

- 24 percent all-beef
- 64 percent combination beef and pork
- 12 percent poultry.

In 1997, consumers bought 850 million pounds of hot dogs at retail stores. Almost 20 percent of these hot dogs were fat-free and light brands. Hot dogs sold in restaurants, stands, and ballparks, of course, also account for a big chunk of the 2 billion pounds manufactured annually. Other markets include school lunch programs, institutional sales, the military, and exports.

Hot dogs are a big business. In 1997, retail sales of hot dogs were approximately $1.5 billion. Almost half those sales were made between May and August. The average American household buys 7.65 pounds of hot dogs annually at a cost of $12.55.

The All-American Hot Dog

The name "hot dog" was invented by T. A. Dorgan, a cartoonist, as an abbreviated version of "red hot dachshund dog" which frank vendors yelled out in ball parks at the time.

This practice originated on a cold April day in 1901 at the New York Polo Grounds. Because of the chill in the air, concessionaire Harry Stevens was not selling much ice cream or cold soda. He thought: What about serving something hot? Soon, his vendors were selling hot dogs from portable hot water tanks. "They're red hot!" vendors cried. "Get your dachshund sausages while they're red hot."

Sitting in the press box, Dorgan heard and saw the vendors—and inspiration struck. He drew a cartoon of a barking dachshund sausage sitting in a roll. Because he wasn't sure how to spell "dachshund," he instead wrote as a caption "hot dog!" And the term hot dog was born.

Now hot dogs are a staple in baseball stadiums throughout the country. The first team to serve hot dogs in its stadium was the St. Louis Browns in 1893, owned at the time by Chris Von de Ahe, a St. Louis bar owner. Legend has it that Babe Ruth once ate 12 hot dogs between games of a doubleheader.

Baseball even gave one brand of hot dogs—Ball Park Franks—its name. In 1957, the owner of the Detroit Tigers selected a premium frankfurter made by Hygrade to serve in its stadium. The premium frank proved so popular that Hygrade packaged it for sale in supermarkets as the "Ball Park Frank." The advertising slogan: "They plump when you cook 'em." TV commercials showed Ball Park Frank hot dogs actually expanding and getting plumper as they were cooked.

Each year, 26 million hot dogs are served in major league stadiums. That's enough hot dogs to stretch from New York to California—or to circle the bases of a Major League ballpark 36,000 times. To look at it another way, for every five tickets sold, two hot dogs are purchased. Dodger Stadium in Los Angeles serves more franks than any other major league ballpark in the country—over 2 million annually.

The *Sporting News*, a magazine covering baseball, announced plans in 1998 to offer a chain of Sporting News Grille theme restaurants. One of the executives in charge is Bill Handwerker, grandson of Nathan Handwerker, founder of Nathan's Coney

Island hot dog emporium in 1916. Ironically, the *Sporting News* management team, which wants a more upscale restaurant, will serve steak rather than hot dogs.

The name hot dog caught on and its usage has expanded far beyond baseball. The slang name for the Olympic sport of freestyle skiing is "hot dogging." A person who is reckless or a risk-taker is sometimes called a "hot dog." The expression "Hot dog!" is often used to indicate enthusiasm or happiness. In 1957, the U.S. Chamber of Commerce officially designated July as National Hot Dog Month.

In June 1996, the National Hot Dog & Sausage Council of the American Meat Institute issued a press release stating its (mainly) tongue-in-cheek guidelines for proper cooking, serving, and eating of hot dogs. Among their "rules":

- Don't put hot dog toppings between the hot dog and the bun. Put the condiments on top of the dog, not on the bun.
- Acceptable buns: plain, poppy, or sesame seed.
- Use a paper napkin. Cloth is too upscale. Serve the hot dog on a paper plate. Everyday dishes are also acceptable; china is again too upscale.
- Eat hot dogs on buns with your hands. Do not use utensils.
- Don't take more than five bites to finish a hot dog of average size. For foot-long wieners, seven bites are okay.
- Acceptable beverages to drink with hot dogs: beer, soda, lemonade, iced tea. Wine is too pretentious.
- Don't leave bits of bun on your plate. Finish every bite.

To observe the last guideline, it's important to serve the right bun with the right dog. Don't serve a 12-inch bun with an 8-inch dog and expect your guests to fill up on the extra bread. The reverse, a hot dog that's too long for the bun, is rarely a problem for the hot dog enthusiast, who feels like he's getting "extra dog" for his money.

"I Wish I Were an Oscar Mayer Wiener"

Just as hot dogs are an integral part of American culture, so are advertising slogans. Examples that come to mind include Maxwell House's "Good to the Last Drop," Morton Salt's "When It Rains, It Pours," and of course Oscar Mayer's "I Wish I Were an Oscar Mayer Wiener."

Oscar Mayer was founded by two brothers, Oscar and Gottfried Mayer, who immigrated to the United States from Germany. Gottfried had been a sausage maker and ham curer in Germany; Oscar worked in the U.S. in the Chicago stockyards.

When Oscar arrived in America in 1873, he was 14 years old. He joined family members in Detroit, where he immediately went to work in a meat shop.

In 1883, the brothers leased the Kolling Meat Market, a small store in a German neighborhood on the north side of Chicago. Their specialties included bratwurst, liverwurst, and weiswurst, a mixture of pork, veal, eggs, and spices. Pork was selling for 8 to 12 cents a pound, and on their first day of business, they grossed $59 in sales. Soon Oscar's salesmen could be seen carrying large orders in wicker baskets out of the neighborhood.

A few years later, they expanded their business into a two-story market they built only a few blocks from the original location. Oscar and Gottfried lived in apartments over the new store along with a third brother, Max, who became the bookkeeper. Deliveries were made in horse-drawn wagons to customers throughout Chicago and the surrounding suburbs.

By 1883, Oscar Mayer and Company employed 43 people, including five salesmen, one pig cleaner, and two stablemen who took care of the delivery horses. However, Oscar's breakthrough business idea was *branding*.

At the time, most meat packagers did not put brand markings on their products. In 1904, Oscar Mayer officially created the Oscar Mayer label and brands for all the meats the store sold. In 1906, when the Food Safety Inspection Service (FSIS) was created to inspect food processors and sellers for purity, Oscar Mayer was among the first to submit to the inspections, thus becoming one of the first recognized, federally approved meat brands.

In 1929, Oscar Mayer began wrapping each hot dog with a yellow paper band. The band was imprinted with the brand name and U.S. government inspection stamp. At the time, most hot dogs were sold in bulk, unpackaged, from a display box. With the band, the consumer would always know she was buying an Oscar Mayer wiener. In 1944, the firm purchased a machine that could automatically wrap the bands around each dog, savings hours of tedious hand-wrapping.

The jingle featuring the line "I Wish I Were an Oscar Mayer Wiener" was introduced in a TV commercial in 1963, and is still in use today:

Oh I wish I were an Oscar Mayer Wiener.
That is what I'd truly like to be.
Cause if I were an Oscar Mayer Wiener.
Everyone would be in love with me.

Thousands of children know this song. Eventually it became so famous it was performed by the Vienna Symphony Orchestra.

In 1989, Oscar Mayer merged with Kraft Foods, one of the largest food companies in North America.

Oscar Mayer is also famous for its Wienermobiles, a fleet of hot dog trucks resembling giant hot dogs on wheels. The Wienermobile was one of the early examples of vehicle-based advertising. Nowadays, many advertisers paint cars or vans with promotional messages and slogans.

In 1936, Carl Mayer, Oscar's nephew, came up with the idea for the Wienermobile. The first Wienermobile was built by the General Body Company of Chicago. It was a 13-foot hot dog on wheels with open cockpits in the center and rear.

Eight different short men drove it, playing the character of Little Oscar, the world's smallest chef. One of them was Meinhardt Raabe, who played a Munchkin in the classic movie *The Wizard of Oz*.

The 1950s models consisted of a 22-foot-long hot dog mounted on a Dodge chassis. The 1958 model was the first Wienermobile to have the hot dog mounted on a bun, which covered a Jeep chassis.

In 1988, six 23-foot-long fiberglass hot dogs on wheels were built. The drivers were referred to as "Hotdoggers," and the cars as "Lamborwienies" or "Wienebagos." They featured microwave ovens, refrigerators, cellular phones, and stereo systems that played 21 versions of the Oscar Mayer jingle.

The latest model, unveiled in 2000, is 27 feet long and 11 feet high. It comes equipped with video equipment, a big-screen TV monitor, and a hot-dog-shaped dashboard and glove-box. Top speed is in excess of 90 miles an hour. Six of these Wienermobiles are on the road with license plates naming them YUMMY, WEENR, BIG BUN, HOT DOG, OUR DOG, and OSCAR. More than a thousand people apply each year to drive one of these six Wienermobiles, out of which 12 are hired.

Hot Dogs Overseas

The hot dog started in Europe, became a traditional American food, and is now gaining popularity overseas again as Russia and China import made-in-the-U.S.A. wieners in record amounts.

According to the National Hot Dog and Sausage Council, which tracks hot dog and sausage consumption trends for the American meat and poultry industry, the leading overseas customer by far is the Russian Federation. Since the end of the Cold War in 1991, Russians have developed a huge taste for the American hot dog.

At a time when livestock production in Russia has fallen behind during the restructuring of the economy, Russian consumers are turning to U.S. hot dogs as a major source of protein and are eating American franks for breakfast, lunch, and dinner. As a result, the Russian market for U.S. hot dogs has skyrocketed—from $122,000 in sales in 1992 to over $70 million in 1996.

Behind this dramatic growth in sales, the Council explains that "sosiska" or sausage has always been routine fare in Russia. For breakfast, Russians slice hot dogs, fry them in butter, and dish them up with bread, cheese, and smoked fish.

At the same time, Russians consider hot dogs the perfect metro station snack food which has led to an explosion of hot dog stands—one on almost every corner in the downtown areas.

The Russian love affair with "sosiska" goes back to a time when there were no imported products, no buns, and a shortage of paper products for plates and napkins. During these Cold

War days, consumers ate their hot dog on a single slice of bread—sometimes white, sometimes Russian black bread, sometimes fresh, but often stale—with a squirt of watered-down ketchup.

Now, reports the Council, American hot dogs are widely available and are being featured in a variety of presentations. Along with the basic hot dog and bun combination served with the option of different condiments, vendors now dress up American wieners and sell them as fancy food.

For example, a top seller at $2 each—compared to 50 cents for the common-variety imported hot dog—is "Po-Fransusky" (French style), which is served in a simulated baguette. Here, vendors bore a hole in the bread; squirt ketchup, mustard, or mayonnaise inside; and then insert a long, skinny hot dog into the middle. Sales of "Po Fransusky" are strong, as are a variety of dressed-up sausages, brats, and wursts.

Besides dressing up their hot dogs, the Russians prefer more spicy franks than do Americans. As a result, hot dogs manufactured for the Russian market contain a lot more garlic. Further, Russians buy a lot of American-made poultry hot dogs because overseas shipping costs put beef and pork franks out of the price range of most consumers.

"It is clear from U.S. export statistics that American hot dogs have found true popularity in the Russian marketplace," said J. Patrick Boyle, president of the American Meat Institute (AMI). "In five short years, American franks have become mainstream in the Russian culture, because they have been adapted to suit Russian taste preferences and eating habits."

Hot dogs are also big in China. American franks are mostly consumed by younger Chinese and the well-to-do, but U.S. manufacturers are looking at what is possible in the near future: in Beijing alone, there are 10 million potential consumers who are already biting into American fast food and are anxious for more options.

China has a population of 1.3 billion, the largest of any nation in the world. According to *The Kiplinger Letter*, China will become the top export market for the U.S. by 2013. As the Chinese economy is booming, more and more Chinese are becoming affluent. These affluent Chinese consumers eat more red meat than poor Chinese, whose diet is mostly fish, rice, chicken, and vegetables.

The potential Asian market for franks is so great that at least one major U.S. company is building hot dog manufacturing plants in China, with other companies eyeing the market carefully. Over 450 U.S. companies are now based in China—more than ten times the number of American companies there in 1990. They employ 250,000 people and have combined annual sales of $23 billion.

In selling to China, U.S. marketers are quickly learning to adapt to the Chinese way of eating hot dogs which, in a word, is unique. The popular sensation is "Rouchang," a fully cooked, cold hot dog wrapped in red plastic which the Chinese eat like a Popsicle, slowly peeling the red plastic down as they go. Sold in supermarkets, food stands, and on the street, "Rouchang" is eaten cold and taken everywhere as a snack.

Also coming into its own is the warmed hot dog which vendors serve on a stick. In this version, Chinese consumers eat the hot dog solo—without a bun or any condiments.

American hot dog exporters have learned that Chinese consumers like their hot dogs sweet. And like their Russian counterparts, the Chinese are fond of franks made from poultry—although hot dogs are also selling in beef, pork, mixed meat and pepperoni varieties.

Franks in the Bedroom

Now on to a sensitive topic: hot dogs in sex. Actually, despite its phallic shape, the hot dog is conspicuously absent from sex histories, how-to manuals, films, and urban legends.

One notable exception was a policeman in Staffordshire, England. He came home from the night shift early one morning in 1995 and saw his wife making breakfast. As a joke, he pulled out his penis, wrapped it in a slice of bread, and offered it to her.

Unfortunately, his pet dog, a large Labrador, thought it was a hot dog in a roll. He leaped over and took a quick hungry bite... and the officer fell rolling to the floor.

The policeman was rushed to a nearby hospital where surgeons repaired the damage. His buddies at the station were anxiously waiting to see how he filled out his medical claims form.

According to dream experts, there's no sexual meaning to seeing a hot dog or sausage in your dreams, either. If you dream of making sausage, it means you will be successful in many undertakings. If you dream of eating them, you will have a humble but pleasant home.

Chapter 3:

How Is a Hot Dog Made?

This chapter explains how cattle are transformed into hot dogs, showing the various processes used at every step from farm to fork. It also lists and describes the various ingredients used by different food processors. Oscar Mayer has one of the most modern plants, with a continuous automated process that makes 38,000 franks an hour.

Where's the Beef?

Why do civilized men, women, and children eat the slaughtered carcasses of animals less intelligent than themselves? A recent article in *Scientific American* (June, 2004) suggests that our ability to thrive on a meat diet, despite such drawbacks as cholesterol and bacteria, may be genetic in nature.

For early man, meat supplied more calories, protein, and nutrients than he could get from gathering fruits, nuts, and leafy greens. Despite the fact that we are the most feared and dangerous predator on the planet, we are physically among the weakest of animals. To obtain his meat, early man had to evolve a bigger brain capable of planning hunting strategies and devising weapons able to bring down animals stronger, tougher, and faster than himself. In essence, the need to eat meat may have been the driving force in our evolution from cave man to 21st-century man!

Let's say you were craving a hot dog, lived on a farm, and all major brand manufacturers were on strike. If you were the resourceful type, you could make your own hot dog. And of course you'd start with a cow.

There are no cows raised specifically for hot dogs, but there are cows raised specifically for beef. The ideal selection is a steer or heifer in the age range of 30 months to 5 years.

You can use younger or older animals. The disadvantage of an older steer is less tasty meat. But for a hot dog, where the meat is ground, chopped, and spiced, this is less critical than for a steak or other cut of unprocessed meat.

Boyd Adelman, a spokesperson for Sabrett, says the company prefers to use bull meat in its hot dogs: "Bull meat is leaner, about 95 percent lean. It gives us a higher-protein product with a good bite." The bull meat is mixed with "choice trimmings," largely the fatty outer layers of the beef, to produce a hot dog that is about 22 percent fat.

During the last 60 days of its life, the cow or bull is confined to a stall and fed corn to fatten it up, hence the term "corn-fed beef." The more you fatten up the animal prior to butchering, the better the quality of the meat.

The details of the butchering are not pleasant, but they are a part of the truth about how the meat gets from the barn into your hot dog roll.

The fact is, everyone who eats meat should be aware of how they get their food. Hunting enthusiasts say that anti-hunting activists who eat meat are hypocritical, and if you are familiar with slaughterhouses, you can see their point of view. Likewise, you can also make a case for hypocrisy in animal rights activists who are not vegetarians.

Food is withheld from the animal for 24 hours prior to slaughter, although it is given water to drink. The reason to stop feeding is to reduce the weight and volume when removing the organs during butchering.

The cow or bull becomes meat when the farmer or slaughterhouse worker kills the animal. Some farmers kill the animal by shooting it with a gun. Others stun the cow or bull by hitting it in the head with a striking hammer. Then the throat is cut to sever the jugular vein and carotid arteries, which quickly kills the animal.

If this description horrifies you but not to the point where you are willing to give up carnivorous pleasures, take solace in the knowledge that more and more farmers and slaughterhouse workers are being taught to butcher humanely. Even then, though, the motive is often for the benefit of the livestock producer and processor, not the cow or bull: if the animal becomes frightened, it causes a release of adrenaline which some experts believe adversely affects the quality of the meat. Also, fear can cause the animal to struggle, which can damage some of the prime cuts as well as pose a danger to the workers.

Urban legends abound about the allegedly vile ingredients used in making hot dogs—rat droppings, chicken beaks, cow eyeballs. But the meat in a hot dog is basically ground beef, and ground beef is basically the same cow meat used in filet mignon, sirloin steak, flank steak, and other choice cuts.

When a cow or bull is butchered, it is cut up, using knives and perhaps a meat saw, into different cuts: ribs, pot roast, sirloin steak, flank steak, rump roast, T-bone, and Porterhouse steaks. This is not a neat operation. There are plenty of pieces left over too small to sell as steaks or roasts. These become hamburger or hot dog meat.

The ground beef used in hamburgers and hot dogs ideally has four parts of lean meat to one part of fat. Ground beef with higher fat content will not freeze well, since fat is difficult to freeze.

How to Make a Hot Dog

Although each manufacturer has their own proprietary process, the average hot dog is made with simple ingredients: meat, salt, sugar, and spices.

One meat processing handbook for food service professionals suggests that you start with 100 pounds of meat, half beef, and half trimmed pork. Grind the meat through ¾-inch plates.

Keep track of how much lean vs. fatty meat you grind for your mixture. Aim for 29 percent fat content (food processors have techniques for measuring fat content that need not concern us here).

Chop the lean trim meat first in a cutter with ice, salt, sugar, ¼-ounce sodium nitrite, ¼-ounce sodium erythrobate, 4 ounces white pepper, 2 ounces each ginger and nutmeg, and 1 ounce each of onion powder and garlic powder. Chopping with ice should continue until the temperature of the mixture reaches 40 degrees Fahrenheit.

Then add fat to the chopper. Chop under vacuum. The goal is to get the mixture thick enough to stuff into casings. You may need to add an emulsifier to achieve the desired consistency.

The hot dog mix is stuffed into cellulose casings and then transferred to a commercial smokehouse. The hot dogs are smoked for about an hour at temperatures ranging from 129 to 176 degrees Fahrenheit.

After smoking, the hot dogs are placed in a cooler and chilled to a temperature of 37 degrees Fahrenheit, which is five degrees above freezing. The idea is to firm the meat to the point where the casings can be peeled away while the hot dogs hold their shape.

Just before peeling, the hot dogs can be placed in the smoke house and exposed to scalding steam for one to two minutes. This loosens the casing (dry casings are much more difficult to peel). The casings are then removed using a mechanical peeler. The hot dogs are vacuum-packed for best retention of quality, and shipped refrigerated for retail distribution and consumption.

Inside a Typical Hot Dog Plant

In most food processing plants, hot dogs are made primarily of pork and beef trimmings. The meat is cut into small pieces and, with ice, put in an emulsifier, a type of mixer. Spices are also added to the mix. So is sodium phosphate, a binder, and sodium nitrite, a preservative (sodium nitrate is also sometimes used as a preservative).

Stainless-steel chopping blades blend the meat, spice, and ice mix into a batter, also called an emulsion. In most emulsifiers, the blades do not move; instead, the bowl spins, sending the mix into the stationary blades.

The batter, which looks like pink bread dough, is transferred into a steel bin. The bin is raised and emptied into an automatic stuffer/linker machine. Workers attach casings to injection tubes (called horns). Batter flows through the tubes into the casings, filling them.

The manufacturer can use natural or cellulose casings. Natural casings, made from cleaned and processed intestines, are left on the dog when it is cooked and eaten, giving it a snap or crunch that many dog aficionados enjoy—especially when a natural-casing dog is deep fried. Cellulose casings are typically removed, resulting in the skinless hot dogs sold in supermarkets.

Once the casings are filled, workers pull them off the tubes and tie off the ends. A fresh empty casing is put over the tube and the process repeated.

The filled casing is fed through another tube, called the linker. As the name implies, the linker ties off the casings in sections of preset length to make individual hot dogs. But the hot dogs are not yet cut, and remain together in a link. A typical filled casing is 12 to 15 feet long, so it will be made into 24 to 30 franks.

The uncut links are put on a conveyor belt and transferred to the smokehouse, where workers hang them in loops on steel racks called "smoke trees" because of their tree-like shape.

Smoking for modern hot dog processing is quick, taking only a couple of hours at most. In the smokehouse, the meat is surrounded by smoke from burning wood or sawdust. The smoke reacts with the sodium nitrite to give hot dogs a darker red color and smoky flavor. Some hot dog makers may add additional flavorings or follow smoking with simmering, too.

After smoking, the hot dogs are rinsed, cooled, and packaged. If they are skinless, they are first sent to an automatic peeler which removes the cellulose casing.

Hot dogs sold retail are usually separated into individual dogs. Hot dogs sold in delis may be left in links. The entire manufacturing process—from putting the cut meat in the bowl to loading the packaged hot dogs on a truck for delivery—takes only a few hours.

Hot dogs on the market today can contain beef, pork, chicken, and sometimes veal. Dogs sold as "skinless" either have the casing removed or a natural cellulose casing. Regular (non-skinless) dogs have a skin that is often a meat casing, such as a washed and salted intestine.

There are a variety of sizes. "Regular" franks come nine to ten links per pound. Dinner franks come approximately five per pound. In cocktail franks, there are 26 to 28 miniature links per pound.

If the package says "all meat," then the hot dog is made from selected cuts of shoulder, flank, loin, and other skeletal meats. If a package is not marked "all meat," then the beef is probably diluted with extenders or fillers, such as milk powder, cereal, and soy flour. It also likely contains less desirable parts of the cow or bull, such as the heart, liver, or tongue—although to be fair, many people, including my mother, think tongue is a delicacy and pay premium prices for it at their local delicatessen.

Taste is controlled in part through choice of meats and selection of spices. Pure beef hot dogs are the zestiest. Those using chicken, pork, or veal are milder. Using extenders such as cereal or dry milk makes the taste milder and the texture softer.

Spice selection can include allspice, anise, bay leaves, caraway, cardamom, cassia, celery seed, cinnamon, cloves, coriander, cumin, garlic, ginger, lemon juice, mace, marjoram, mustard seed, nutmeg, onion, paprika, pepper, sage, salt, and thyme.

Make Your Own Hot Dogs

A hot dog is of course a sausage, and some people make sausages at home. Can you make a hot dog at home, using a scaled-down version of the above process? I suppose so, theoretically. I haven't tried it. But what if you wanted to?

To begin with, you need a meat grinder for your kitchen. Look for a grinder specifically designed for making sausage. It should come equipped with a variety of plates as well as an attachment for stuffing the meat into casings.

You also need to buy casings. A hank or bundle contains approximately 100 yards of casing, into which you can stuff approximately 100 to 125 pounds of meat. For home-made hot dogs, the most popular casings are lamb and sheep casings.

There is a big variety of other casings available. Animal casings include hog and beef. Cellulose casings are made from a special grade of cotton linters. The linters are dissolved into a solution and then reformed into casings. Casings are also made out of muslin, fibers, and even collagen, a gelatinous substance found in the connective tissue, bones, and cartilage of mammals.

For home hot dog making, seven-bone roast, blade cut roast, pot roast, or anything from the chuck or shoulder of beef works fine. The meat should be about one-fourth fat, three-quarters lean.

For pork, Boston butt or shoulder has this correct ration of three-quarters lean and one-quarter fat.

The meat should be refrigerated before grinding, and cut into strips small enough to fit in your grinder. Keeping the meat cold prevents contamination and spoilage, but it also achieves another important goal: making the beef and pork as stiff as possible without freezing. If the meat is too soft, grinding crushes it and causes the juices to run out, resulting in a dry hot dog. Firm meat retains the juices even after grinding.

Spices can be added before or after grinding. You can mix the spices with the cut-up meat and then place it in the grinder. Or you can grind the meat; then mix in the spices.

When my mother made home-made meat balls when I was a child, she allowed us to taste the raw beef mix before cooking. When making hot dogs using ground beef and pork, don't taste the mixture, and wash your hands thoroughly afterward. Raw pork can give you trichinosis, an unpleasant and dangerous gastrointestinal illness.

Probably the easiest way to make home-made sausage of any kind is to add the spice to the meat first, then grind it. That way, what comes out of the grinder is ready to stuff into the casing.

You slip the casing over the exit spout of the grinder. Use water as a lubricant to help the casing go over this nozzle or "stuffing horn." Force some meat through the casing, and then push the rest of the meat back into the horn. You now have a section of empty casing adjacent to the horn, followed by a section filled with meat.

As the hot dogs are formed, you can tie the ends or make links. Links are formed by twisting the stuffed casing at various intervals as it comes off the stuffing horn.

One recipe for home-made hot dogs calls for 3 pounds of fine ground beef chuck, 2 pounds of fine ground pork butt, 2 teaspoons of white pepper, 1 teaspoon of ground coriander, 1 teaspoon of ground ginger, 1 teaspoon of ground mace, 4 cloves of pressed garlic, 1½ tablespoons of salt, and 1½ cups of water.

The ingredients are mixed well and stuffed into a sheep casing. The hot dogs should then be smoked for two to three hours at 115 degrees Fahrenheit in an electric smoker, or until the links are rich orange in color. Then cook the hot dogs in water heated to 170 degrees Fahrenheit. They're done when you see them floating on the surface.

Chicken Franks

I can't understand why anyone would eat other than a beef or beef-and-pork frank. You eat hot dogs because they taste good, not because they're health food. Beef franks taste the best. Chicken franks are bland and unsatisfying.

Yet there is a trend today to produce low-fat or no-fat, low-salt or no-salt, and low-cholesterol or no-cholesterol versions of foods that are normally loaded with fat, salt, and cholesterol. You can buy fake eggs, meatless breakfast sausages, fat-free milk, and other foods which are carefully formulated to taste like the originals but don't.

Hot dogs are no exception, and if you're eating chicken these days instead of red meat, you could substitute chicken when making your own hot dogs.

Start with three feet of hog or sheep casings, one and a half inches in diameter. Rinse clean under cold water. Soak in a bowl of cool water while you are preparing the meat.

A wet casing is much easier to stuff and place over the grinder horn than a dry one. To make the casing even more pliable, add a splash of white vinegar to the bowl of cold water while the casing is soaking.

Before stuffing, slip the casing over the kitchen faucet and run cold water through it to flush out any excess salt.

Grind three pounds of chicken meat mixed with the following spices: a tablespoon of onion powder; one and a half teaspoons of salt; a teaspoon each of finely ground coriander, paprika, white pepper, sugar, and garlic powder; and half a teaspoon each of dried marjoram, ground mace, and finely ground mustard seed.

To give your home-made chicken franks the consistency of commercial hot dogs treated with emulsifiers, put the meat and seasoning in a food processor and process until the mixture is a thick puree-like consistency.

Stuff the casings and twist off into five-inch links. Simmer in a pot of water for half an hour. Remove the franks and chill them thoroughly in ice water. Remove, pat dry, and refrigerate. The chicken dogs can be stored up to a week in your refrigerator.

The Kosher Frank

To many hot dog lovers, nothing beats the flavor of a kosher frank. According to the National Hot Dog and Sausage Council, 14 million pounds of kosher hot dogs are sold each year.

The word "kosher" is used in Jewish tradition to indicate that a food is approved for consumption. Food that is "fit to eat," according to Hebrew dietary laws, is kosher. The Bible (Leviticus 11:3 and 11:7) specifies which animals can be eaten: "Whatsoever parteth the hoof, and is cloven-footed and cheweth the cud, among the beasts, that shall ye eat. And the swine, though he divideth the hoof, and be clovenfooted, yet he cheweth not the cud; he is unclean unto you."

Manufacturing a kosher meat product requires using animals without disease or blemishes, and processing the meat using proper and humane methods. Only the forequarter of cattle is used, and the beef is processed within 72 hours. Food certified as kosher has been inspected by a rabbi.

And there are other requirements:

- The animal must be killed by a *shohet*—a specially trained, ritual slaughterer—in the most painless and humane way possible.
- A *bodek*, or trained inspector, checks the animal's organs immediately after slaughter to ensure wholesomeness. There are 70 defects that can cause an animal to be rejected. These include perforated or punctured organs, internal cuts and bruises, hernias, and bone fractures.
- Certain blood vessels, nerves, and lobes of fat forbidden by Jewish dietary law are removed from the carcass and the blood fully drained (the Bible forbids the consumption of blood, which is why Dracula never buys kosher foods).
- The meat is washed, soaked in water, and salted with coarse kosher salt. Kosher salt has larger grains than ordinary table salt, so it adheres better to the meat.

National Foods is the largest kosher meat processor in the United States. The company, famous for its Hebrew National brand hot dogs, processes and distributes kosher meat, poultry, and delicatessen products, both bulk and packaged. These products—which include salami, bologna, knockwurst, sausage, tongue, corned beef, pastrami, turkey, chicken, sauerkraut, pickles, and mustard—are available nationwide under a variety of brand names including Zion, Galil, Schorr's, Rosoff, Mogen David, and Isaac Gellis.

Hebrew National is one of the best-known and most popular brands of kosher hot dog. The Hebrew National hot dog is the only frankfurter served at the James Beard Foundation, a prestigious culinary institute. In June 1995, *Good Housekeeping* ranked the Hebrew National beef frank as one of the top 12 hot dogs, making the following comment: "Real beefy aroma and taste; garlicky and spicy with a nice chewiness; coarsely textured; very juicy."

National Foods was founded in 1905 as the "Hebrew National Kosher Sausage Factory, Inc." Hebrew National made kosher meats—then commonly known as "delicatessen"—for New York deli restaurants. The company's first facility was located in a six-story walk-up building on East Broadway on New York's Lower East Side. Sales were both direct and through jobbers, with distribution highly concentrated among the Jewish community. Hebrew National was the trusted kosher brand for many newly settled Eastern European and German Jewish immigrants in the New York area.

Availability of affordable kosher meat was of critical importance in those days to Jewish families living on the Lower East Side. When meat sellers raised the price of kosher beef from 12 to 18 cents a pound in 1902, there were literally riots in the streets. Jewish women smashed windows, wrecked butcher shops, overturned pushcarts, picketed, and assaulted both consumers and cops who interfered with their picket lines.

Isidore Pines purchased Hebrew National in 1928. Under Pines, the business remained solvent through the stock market crash of 1929 and the Great Depression that followed. When Pines died in 1936, his 22-year-old son Leonard became president and moved the company headquarters to Brooklyn.

During the 1940s, Hebrew National increased revenues by expanding the market for kosher meats beyond ethnic neighborhoods. The company introduced its products into the newly booming suburban marketplace beyond New York City, and began creating packaged products specifically for supermarket sales. In 1960, Leonard Pines changed the name of the company from Hebrew National Kosher Sausage Factory, Inc. to Hebrew National Kosher Foods, Inc.

In 1968, Houston-based Riviana Foods bought a controlling interest in Hebrew National, and in 1976, Colgate-Palmolive purchased Riviana Foods. Four years later, Leonard Pines' son, Skip Pines, bought the Hebrew National company back from Colgate-Palmolive.

Although hot dogs are not thought of as a health food, kosher products are, in certain aspects, healthier than non-kosher foods. The main ingredients in Hebrew National hot dogs are beef, water, salt, spices, garlic powder, and paprika. No artificial colorings, flavorings, or fillers are used.

Consumer preference for kosher dogs, combined with a series of acquisitions in the 1980s, contributed to significant growth. In 1986, Hebrew National changed its name to National Foods to incorporate new brands added under these acquisitions.

In 1993, ConAgra, Inc., a multi-national food conglomerate, acquired the stock in National Foods, which continues to operate as an independent company. The firm manufactures pickles in Hunts Point, New York, and processes beef and poultry products in Indianapolis, Indiana. The company also owns a meat processing plant in Miami, Florida.

Chapter 4:

The Hot Dog as an American Icon

Hot dogs, along with baseball games and apple pie, are a part of the American culture. This chapter examines the role the hot dog plays as an American icon. It also looks at hot dogs as both a business and a national pastime, including hot dog eating contests, world's records for hot dog eating, and the world of hot dog vendors.

Americans are expected to eat at least 7 billion hot dogs between Memorial Day and Labor Day, according to the National Hot Dog and Sausage Council, in Arlington, Virginia. Laid end to end, that's enough wieners to stretch from Chicago, in the heartland of America, to the home of the hot dog, in Frankfurt, Germany, 125 times.

The Council estimates that Americans eat 20 billion hot dogs each year, but more are eaten in the warm-weather months when the grills are fired up. If we conservatively estimate the average length at six inches per dog, the total length of these hot dogs, if laid end to end, would be 1,893,939 miles. That's more than three times the distance of a round-trip from the Earth to the moon.

According to 1998 Yankelovich data collected for the Council, 42 percent of Americans said that summer was the best time to eat a hot dog while 34 percent said "any time" was a great time to eat a hot dog.

Many Americans enjoy hot dogs in conjunction with sporting events, because hot dogs are the ultimate hand-held food. Major league baseball fans consume more than 26 million hot dogs while watching games. That's enough wieners to stretch from Fenway Park in Boston to Dodger Stadium in Los Angeles.

To put 26 million hot dogs in perspective, think of enough hot dogs to feed every person in the states of New York and Michigan combined. It's also enough for every man, woman and child in New England to have two hot dogs.

Who will eat the most hot dogs while watching baseball in a given year? Dodger Stadium usually leads the hot dog race with its ever-popular Dodger Dog, 2.2 million of which are sold each season. Jacobs Field in Cleveland sells 1.5 million hot dogs per season, while Oriole Park at Camden Yards in Baltimore estimates that hungry O's fans consume 615,000 hot dogs per season.

As real baseball fans and hot dog aficionados know, no two hot dogs are alike at America's ballparks. Dodger Stadium's best-selling hot dog is the "Dodger Dog," while the "Phanatic Dog" is favored at Veterans Stadium in Philadelphia. Chicagoans watch their beloved Cubs at Wrigley Field while munching on "Chicago Style" dogs, which feature dark yellow mustard, tomato slices, dark green relish, chopped raw onion, and a dash of celery salt on a poppy seed bun. Only at Milwaukee County Stadium (Miller Park) are sausages more popular than hot dogs, with 250,000 bratwursts and 80,000 Polish sausages sold per season.

At Waterfront Park in New Jersey, home of the minor league team the Trenton Thunder, concessionaires sell 1,500 hot dogs per game vs. fewer than 200 hamburgers per game. The favorite is the Thunder Dog, a quarter-pound all-beef frankfurter served with sauerkraut, chili, cheddar, and jalapenos. The hot dogs are grilled on a Rotter Grill, a rack of rotating stainless-steel tubes, each with a heating element inside.

Joe Vitale, a marketing consultant, tells of a hot dog vendor at a ball park who had a problem delivering his dogs. Even though he shouted "hot food coming through," patrons at the ball park would not move out of his way to let him hand the dog to the customer. He then changed his message to "Watch out for the mustard!" and people let him through. Says Vitale, "People know that mustard leaves a stain, and they wanted to avoid getting it on them. That's why they moved."

Hot Dogs in Politics, War, and the Movies

On July 22, 1998, a special luncheon was held for more than 1,000 Capitol Hill staff, lawmakers, and federal agency personnel in Washington, DC. The subject of the celebration? July as National Hot Dog month.

The main course was 4,300 hot dogs—enough to circle the Capitol dome four times. Also served: 1,000 bottled waters, 840 sodas, 840 beers, 800 bags of Utz potato chips, 275 pounds of baked beans, 60 pounds of chili, 600 Hostess Twinkies and Cupcakes, and 1,000 boxes of Cracker Jack.

Two years earlier, during National Hot Dog Month in 1996, U.S. troops in Bosnia had gotten a big airlift from hot dog and other fast-food makers through Operation Wienerlift, organized by the National Hot Dog and Sausage Council. More than 37,000 hot dogs, 700 pounds of mustard, 15,000 boxes of Cracker Jack, and 3,500 pounds of beef summer sausage departed Dover Air Force Base July 21st bound for Bosnia in an effort to sustain the high morale among troops in Bosnia.

"While we can't send a major league ball team to Bosnia, we can send the foods that are enjoyed most in balls parks and at picnics and backyard barbecues," said National Hot Dog and Sausage Council President J. Patrick Boyle. "We owe the troops a debt of gratitude for their sacrifice, and we hope this shipment gives them a taste of home for a day."

Next stop for the hot dog along the progression of American popular culture is a feature film, *Footlong*. In 1998, Chris Patak and Gerry Beyer, two New Jersey filmmakers, bought a red '82 Chevy van, bolted a home-made, five-foot wooden frankfurter to the roof, and began making their way across the country to make a documentary about hot dogs, titled *Footlong*.

To Patak, 27, and Beyer, 28, the frank is not so much a food as it is the quintessential symbol of America. More than Mount Rushmore, the White House, or even baseball, it is, they say, a national icon that inspires patriotic fervor and captures the indomitable American spirit.

"It affects [people's] lives in big ways," says Patak. "People get really animated about hot dogs. Once you get them talking about hot dogs, it's hard to shut them up."

During filming, their oddly accessorized van drew a lot of attention. In Chicago, a bunch of women in bikinis and Rollerblades followed them through town.

In Los Angeles, they interviewed 89-year-old Charlie Kazan, who, since childhood, has suffered from a rare digestive disorder that has prevented him from eating anything but hot dogs and fried baloney sandwiches. Just about every meal consists of a plain hot dog on two slices of bread and a cup of coffee. "He's never been sick a day in his life," says Beyer. "And he's not sick of eating hot dogs at all."

In Columbus, Ohio, they met John Mowery, who, for the past four years, has run the Hot Dog Ministry. The moviemakers spent a day watching Mowery cook 350 hot dogs in his tiny kitchen and then distribute them to the homeless as he preached the gospel. "They love him," Patak says of central Ohio's homeless. "A lot of them come just for the food, but some of them pray with him."

In St. Louis, they found a member of a Banana Seat Bike Club whose seat was shaped nothing like the yellow fruit. The man's cycle had the requisite two wheels and handlebars all right, but riders sat on a roughly eight-foot-long hot dog made of wire, vinyl, and Styrofoam.

The trek also took the duo to places such as Usinger's, a sausage factory in Milwaukee; Kasper's in Oakland, California, which cooks its own condiments instead of taking them from a jar; Callahan's in Fort Lee, New Jersey, which deep-fries its dogs; and Pink's in Los Angeles, a roadside stand that serves 25 varieties. "Hot dogs represent a predictability of life; everything changes, but the hot dog remains the same," Pink's owner, Gloria Pink, says. "It's a comfort food that crosses all socioeconomic levels. It's like returning home."

Pink's is probably the most famous hot dog stand in the country...certainly in Los Angeles! Located near the corner of Melrose and La Brea, Pink's can be found by looking for a crowd of people and following the aroma of fresh meaty chili and soft hot dog buns.

Pink's is unlike any other hot dog stand in America. For example, it has its own parking lot attendant (parking is free). It has been in the same location for 61 years. It is not unusual to see a Rolls Royce pull up to Pink's (the chili dog ordered will be for the occupant, not the chauffeur). Movie stars, well-known dignitaries, struggling musicians, businessmen, housewives, school children...all have savored Pink's Famous Chili Dogs. Rumor hat it that Orson Welles once at 15 chili dogs at Pink's in one sitting; Bruce Willis proposed to Demi Moore over a Pink's chili dog; and Michael J. Fox used the place as his office.

Other celebrities who have patronized Pink's include *Fraser* star Kelsey Grammer, Bill Cosby, *The West Wing's* John Spencer, Drew Carey, Laurence Fishburne, the casts of the NBC sitcom *Scrubs* and CBS hit show *Everybody Loves Raymond*, Tom Arnold, James Earl Jones, track star Carl Lewis, Steven Tyler of Aerosmith, former California governor Gray Davis, chef Bobby Flay, Carol Channing, Maria Shriver, and Vanna White.

But wait; there's more: Jay Leno, Roseanne, Aaron Spelling, Henry Winkler, rocker David Lee Roth, Mike Ditka of the Chicago Bears, Will Ferrell, Brad Pitt, Jerry Lewis, Jennifer Garner, Jimmy Kimmel, Lionel Richie, and (of course) the singer Pink. Award-winning author Harlan Ellison even immortalized Pink's in his short story, "Prince Myshkin and Hold the Relish," reprinted in the appendix.

Paul Pink started his hot dog stand in 1939. It was only a large-wheeled pushcart in those days. The depression was on and money was scarce. Pink Chili Dogs, complete with a large warm bun, oversized hot dog, mustard, onions, and thick chili sold for ten cents each. His hot dog wagon was located in "the country" among the weeds, rolling hills and open spaces…that was the corner of La Brea and Melrose 61 years ago!

Times have changed, but not at Pink's. In 1946 Paul Pink traded in his hot dog wagon for a small building constructed on the very same spot where the wagon had stood. But the stand hasn't changed since those days.

Today, Pink's Chili Dogs sell for $2.35 each (with inflation and shrinking dollar, they're a better bargain now than in 1939). Pink's still gives that very same quality and quantity: mouth-watering chili, generously topping an all-beef hot dog with mustard and onions. Quality and service — an average Pink's Chili Dog can be ordered, prepared, and delivered to the customer in less than 30 seconds—have been the two reasons Pink's has not only survived, but became famous.

Although the classic is the Pink's chili dog, they have branched out into more exotic fare: The "Millennium Dog" is a foot-long jalapeno sausage topped with hot chili, tomatoes, guacamole, and grilled onions. The newer "Matrix Reloaded" is three slices of cheese melted inside a large tortilla with three grilled beef hot dogs, three strips of bacon, chili, and onions. For the health-minded, there's even a vegetarian "garden dog" made of soy protein, brown sugar, spices, smoke flavor, and egg white solids. Toppings available for the garden dog include mustard, relish, guacamole, onions, coleslaw, and sauerkraut.

To finance their pilgrimage to Pink's and the making of their hot dog movie, Patak and Beyer borrowed money from friends and relatives and pooled their life savings for *Footlong*, which cost more than $1 million to make.

On their road trip in their hot dog van, they ate chili dogs, jalapeno dogs, bacon dogs, and dogs on sticks. They also tried to match bites with former Baltimore Colts lineman Art Donovan, who amazed them with his ability to down as many as 35 dogs in a sitting. And the duo bobbed for wieners at the Hot Dog Festival in Frankfurt, Indiana.

"Sometimes, we'd go four days in a row eating nothing but hot dogs," Patak says, a tad nostalgically. "There were days we'd eat nine hot dogs at nine different places."

Get Your Hot Dogs!

The selling of hot dogs is just as much a tradition as the eating of hot dogs. Hot dog lovers throughout the country are fiercely supportive of their favorite hot dog joints.

There are 3,000 licensed hot dog vendors in New York City alone. The biggest retail outlet for hot dogs is Chicago's O'Hare International Airport, which sells more than 2 million franks a year. The original Nathan's Famous in Coney Island, still in operation after more than 90 years, grosses $70 million annually.

In fact, when Fidel Castro visited the Bronx in 1959, he was photographed by the *Daily News*, at the Bronx Zoo, eating a hot dog.

The nice thing about a hot dog restaurant or stand, other than the casual atmosphere and great eating, is that they are often family affairs. The families run them for decades and get to know each customer by name.

With the low start-up costs, a hot dog stand may be the most inexpensive route to getting into the restaurant business. First-generation hot dog merchants often come from middle-class backgrounds. It is their children who get MBAs and bring in more sophistication when they join the operation.

Anthologists Leonard and Thelma Spinrad tell this story:

A friend said to a man who had a frankfurter stand by the side of the road, "If you put up a sign advertising your stand a mile up the road so people see it before they get here, they might be influenced to stop." He put up a sign and it worked; so as time went on he put up more signs further and further away on the road, and more and more people bought the frankfurters, and the owner was able to send his son to a fine university.

When the son returned he said, "You're spending too much money on your advertising. You don't need those signs." So the father took down some of the signs; the business went down a little, but so did the expense for advertising.

With less business, they decided to cut down a little more on the advertising, and the business went down a little more, until

was put together in such a way that it was a true work of art,' says one former employee who, at age 11, told the owner, Abe Drexler, he was 14 so he could get hired—even though he was not even tall enough to see over the steam counter. 'If you are of the opinion that there is a finer hot dog anywhere, it's only because you have not had a Fluky's.' Frank Sinatra even sings about Fluky's in his song 'Chicago.'"

And of course, Nathan's original stand in Coney Island is still in business serving hot dogs. "There is something about the sea air from the Atlantic Ocean and the dilapidated buildings that give this snappy dog the built-in essence of real life," says one customer.

Occasionally, a vendor finds a new way to promote hot dog sales. The Super Sport Meat Launcher, a machine which costs $7,000, is designed to shoot hot dogs at patrons in ball parks and other venues. The hot dog, along with the bun and packaged condiments, are stuffed in a tube, and then fired at the buyer.

Hot Dog Eating Contests

For nearly 100 years, the United States maintained supremacy in the world of competitive eating. Peter Washburn, Frank Dellarosa, Mike Devito and Ed Krachie are just a few of the heroes who defended the national pride, taking on challengers from all nations of the world in the annual Nathan's Hot Dog Eating Contest in Coney Island.

But during the past few years, America has experienced defeat in this contest. In December, 1996, Hirofumi Nakajima, a 5-foot 6-inch champion from Japan, beat Nathan's world champ Ed Krachie—who stands 6 feet 7 inches and weighs 360 pounds.

Nakajima then successfully defended his title on July 4, 1997, and July 4, 1998, setting a new world record of 24½ hot dogs and buns in 12 minutes. For three years straight, Nakajima returned to Japan and ticker-tape parades with the spoils of victory: the Coveted Mustard Yellow International Belt. The loss of this belt, considered the World Cup of competitive eating, has been a source of embarrassment for American hot dog lovers.

"He is the best I have ever seen," says Krachie of Nakajima. "But America wants to be number one, and nothing is more American than mom, apple pie, and hot dogs." Nakajima, incidentally, says he trains on hamburgers because, he says, "Hot dogs are very expensive in Japan."

What is this annual event like to watch? Each Fourth of July a group of 15 finalists lines up behind a 30-foot table in Sweikert Alley beside Nathan's flagship restaurant on Surf Avenue in Coney Island. At noon, surrounded by spectators and media, the competitors begin the grueling 12-minute contest. They hold several hot dogs and buns in each hand, dip the dogs in seltzer to cool them, and stuff the hot dogs into their mouths.

According to the archives of Nathan's, the Fourth of July Hot Dog Contest was first held in 1916, the year Nathan's opened on Surf Avenue. The contest has been held each year since then, except in 1941, when it was canceled as a protest to the war in Europe, and in 1971, when it was canceled as a protest to civil unrest and the reign of free love.

The 2006 Nathan's Hot Dog Eating Contest was won by Takeru Kobayashi with 53¾ hot dogs in 12 minutes, eclipsing his own 2004 record of 53½. Prior to Kobayashi, the world hot dog eating record was held by Hirofumi Nakajima, also of Japan, who ate 24½ hot dogs in the twelve minute contest on July 4, 1998. Prior to Nakajima, Ed Krachie, a Maspeth, Queens resident, put away 22¼ hot dogs and buns on July 4, 1996, to top the previous record set by Frank "Large" Dellarosa, a fellow Maspeth resident who ate 21½ hot dogs and buns in the 1991 contest. Peter

Washburn, a Brooklyn carnival worker, was the world-record holder prior to this, with 18½ hot dogs and buns.

A very special year for hot dog eating contests was 1993, which marked the return of the coveted Mustard Yellow International Belt to American soil. In November of 1993, in a special one-on-one contest run by TV Tokyo, Nathan's champ Mike Devito beat Japanese eating phenom Orio Ito to reunify the world hot dog eating titles.

There are three hot dog eating titles in the world. The first two—the New York City/Nathan's Hot Dog Eating Council title and the United States Hot Dog Eating Association title—have been held by American champs as long as anyone can remember. However, the Nathan's International Hot Dog Eating Federation title had been held by the Japanese for seven years until Devito brought it home to New York City.

The be-jeweled Mustard Yellow International Belt, worn only by the International Champion, is to hot dog aficionados what the Faberge Eggs were to Czar Nicholas. The belt is of unknown age and value and is unveiled only at the annual contest. With Krachie's loss to Nakajima, the belt was once again taken to Japan, where it stands in a glass case in the Imperial Palace in Kyoto.

Women often compete in the Nathan's Fourth of July Hot Dog Contest. In fact, in the 1950s the contest was won by a German woman, Gerta Hasselhoff, who trained on bratwurst.

Each year, Amos Wengler serenades competitors and fans with his hit number, "Hot Dog," the official anthem of the contest:

Hot dogs, hot dogs,
love to eat 'em up.
Hot dogs, hot dogs,
great with soda pop.
© 1990, Amos Wengler.

Stand-out eating rivalries from the past include Rudman vs. Libnitz, a grudge match that went on for nearly a decade. In the 1930s, Stan Libnitz, from Flushing, Queens, and Andrew Rudman from Brighton Beach, Brooklyn, were the kings of the hot dog eating world. They alternated victories for eight years until Rudman said the 1938 contest would be his last. He vowed to beat Libnitz and settle who was champion once and for all.

At the start of the much-anticipated 1938 contest, Libnitz seemed unsettled. His fans had not arrived and Rudman's cheering section had taken over the crowd.

Nonetheless, six minutes into the contest, Libnitz was two dogs ahead, and at eight minutes he was three and a half dogs ahead. Victory seemed assured. However, that was the point at which Libnitz suddenly stopped eating. Rudman rallied to beat him by one half of a hot dog as Libnitz continually pointed at Rudman's elbow. Following the contest, Libnitz complained bitterly that Rudman had elbowed him in the gut during the contest, and he demanded a rematch.

Rudman agreed, but Libnitz was advised by his doctor that he could not compete again without risking a case of chronic gas. For years, Libnitz complained to anyone who would listen about the events that occurred that day.

U.S. Regains Hot Dog Championship, Then Loses It Again

It was man against dog on a dog-day afternoon. And when it was over, a 317-pound hulk from South Jersey had beaten out the slim reigning champ from Japan to bring the hot dog eating trophy back to the United States.

Steve Keiner, 50, of Egg Harbor Township, was top dog Sunday at Nathan's Famous in Coney Island, Brooklyn, after eating 20¼ hot dogs.

"I took the Zen approach," Keiner said, acknowledging the cultural influence of his competitor, 134-pound Hirofumi Nakajima of Japan, the previous champ. "I went down the path that the hot dog was one with me, and I was one with the universe."

Keiner added: "Could I get some French fries now?"

Nakajima came in fourth, downing just 19 franks. "Hungry" Charles Hardy tied for second with Bartosek Tadeusz, coming within a mouthful of winning with 20 hot dogs under their belts.

As a horde of reporters took his picture, Keiner, an electrical inspector, wrapped himself in the American flag and "We Are the Champions" played on the sound system. The Bunnettes, two perky blondes in sunglasses, boogied by his side.

"There are tears of joy in Coney Island!" said public relations man George Shea, who gave a running commentary throughout what he called a "dogfight" "The belt is back in America!"

"The belt," is a mustard-yellow weight lifter's belt that goes to the winner.

Nakajima seemed sad. "I feel bad, terrible," he said through a translator. "I don't want to look at a hot dog right now."

A former noodle-eating champion, Nakajima, 24, said he was retiring from the world of food-consumption contests. "I'm done," he said. "That's it."

Not everyone was happy to see the slender Japanese man lose. "I feel the drama of it," said spectator Neil Kuslansky. "Here's a guy weighing 130 pounds up against these monsters."

Keiner called Nakajima "an honorable and worthy opponent, but he had to come down. The U.S. had to take it back."

Many of the contestants dipped their hot dogs in water before stuffing them in their faces, but Keiner comes from the purist school. "I tried that once but it ruins the bouquet," he said.

Like spectators at an air show or a racetrack morbidly wondering if disaster is in store, the crowd outside Nathan's watched with slightly nauseous fascination as the 12-minute contest played out.

"I was waiting for someone to vomit," said Stacey Simcox of Queens, as she ate her own hot dog—but just one—after the winner was announced.

And of course, no event in New York is complete without a protest. This one had vegetarians handing out fliers. "It's a pretty disgusting spectacle," said Alex Press of Manhattan. "We love animals."

Nathan's sponsors the contest every July 4th. It was first held in 1916.

Keiner had won a hot dog contest in Philadelphia two weeks earlier, but he insisted that his usual diet excludes high-calorie foods—including hot dogs—and that he exercises regularly.

Most mortals would have a serious case of indigestion after just a fraction of what Keiner downed, but he actually ate a couple more when the contest was over. "I feel great," he said. "And the other thing: They were simply delicious."

On July 4, 2001, Takeru Kobayashi of Japan shattered all previous hot dog eating records by consuming 50 hot dogs and buns in 12 minutes at the Nathan's contest.

In 2002, Kobayashi beat his own record by one half of a hot dog. Like Keiner before him, Kobayashi ate two more franks after the contest while posing for pictures.

Kobayashi's technique is to break the hot dogs in half and shove both pieces in his mouth. He dips the roll in water, balls it up, and swallows it. Like the Japanese hot dog eating champs before him, Kobayashi is a small man—he stands five feet seven inches and weighs 131 pounds. After the contest he weighed 139 pounds, but one assumes he lost that weight after a trip or two to the bathroom.

In the 2000 Nathan's contest in Coney Island, the top three contestants were all Japanese, and all five feet seven inches or under. Their weights were 100, 104, and 187 pounds respectively. They beat out two Americans weighing 355 and 391 pounds.

Ed "The Animal" Krachie, a former champion, has a "belt of fat" theory explaining why the smaller eaters do so well: The skinny eater's stomachs have room to expand, while the heavy eaters have their bellies compressed by fat.

*   *   *

More Hot Dog Americana

- Marlene Dietrich, the actress, said hot dogs and champagne were her favorite meal.
- Babe Ruth once ate 12 hot dogs between games of a doubleheader, and had to be taken to the hospital for indigestion.
- In 1939, U.S. President Franklin Delano Roosevelt served hot dogs to King George IV of England. Years later, Queen Elizabeth II served franks at a royal banquet. Jimmy Carter served them at a White House picnic in 1977.
- Bruce Willis proposed to Demi Moore in front of a hot dog stand.
- Another groom, who also proposed to his wife in front of a hot dog stand, had hot dogs from the stand shipped from New Jersey to Vermont for his pre-wedding dinner.

Chapter 5:

Hot Dogs and Public Safety

Robert Puelo, 32, was apparently being disorderly in a St. Louis market when the clerk threatened to call the police. Puelo grabbed a hot dog, shoved it into his mouth, and walked out without paying. Police found him unconscious in front of the store; paramedics removed the six-inch wiener from his throat, where it had choked him to death.

–Cited in *The Successful Practice* newsletter

We've all heard the rumors about hot dogs: they're made with chicken beaks, cow guts, nails, hair, feces, and all manner of disgusting ingredients. This chapter will explore the history of hot dog making as well as the ingredients used in today's plants. We'll also discuss modern regulation of the meat processing industry including the new mega-regs designed to ensure a safer product.

Some strange behavior surrounds the hot dog industry. On July 6, 2001, a New York City hot dog vendor was arrested by police for washing his underwear in the same pot in which he cooked the hot dogs he sold to consumers.

The United States Department of Agriculture (USDA) budget for regulating meat and poultry is about $800 million a year. They employ 7,600 meat and poultry inspectors, of which 3,000 perform carcass-by-carcass inspections primarily in poultry plants.

Vegan Dogs

There are very few significant major incidents of hot dog contamination and no reports of a widespread hotdog-borne epidemic.

The same cannot be said about beef. As we shall see, the meat industry has a long history of contamination, illness, and impurity.

A number of beef-related concerns—health, nutrition, high fat content, nitrates, cholesterol, cruelty to animals, animal rights—have prompted hordes of people worldwide to turn to a vegetarian diet. Does this mean the pleasures of hot dogs are denied to them forever?

Fortunately no. In 1997, Longalife NotCorn Dogs won "Best of Show" honors at Marketplace '97, the annual convention of the National Nutritional Foods Association. Selected by a panel of more than 160 natural-food retailers as the best-tasting new product, NotCorn Dogs are meatless frankfurters covered with corn batter.

A traditional corn dog, of course, is a regular hot dog dipped and covered with corn batter, and then deep-fried until the corn batter forms a crunchy shell. Corn dogs are often eaten on a stick inserted through the middle of the dog. The corn dog was invented in 1942 for the Texas State Fair by two ex-vaudevillians, Ned and Carl Fletcher.

Where Meat Is Made

The problem die-hard vegetarians have with hot dogs is not one of health or nutrition. It is the fact that, even though it doesn't look like a part of an animal (vs. steak or ribs, which do), a hot dog is made from killing an animal—usually a cow.

We Americans are a nation of carnivores, spending $52 billion a year on beef. "Beef is not some luxury or inessential product, like a cellular phone, that people can take or leave," writes attorney Steven Shaw in *Commentary*. "Especially in the United Kingdom and also in America, it is at the very core of both the food supply and the national consciousness."

Comedienne Sean Morey jokes that vegetarians are hypocrites, and that it is just as cruel to kill a plant as to kill an animal. Both are living things—and, adds Morey, "Animals can run. Plants can't get away."

John Robbins, heir to the Baskin-Robbins fortune and an animal rights activist, responds seriously to this notion. Says Robbins, "It takes 16 pounds of grain to make one pound of beef. It takes one pound of grain to make one pound of bread. So you're consuming fewer plants by eating them directly than you would if you were eating animals, and thus you're allowing more of the biomass of the planet to survive.

"I've harvested cabbages and pulled carrots out of the ground, and I've been in slaughterhouses and seen the animals having their brains bashed out with sledgehammers and their throats cut. The experiences are not comparable. The animals do everything they can to resist: they fight, they scream. They have nervous systems with pain receptors. They have souls. They want to live. I think that plants have group souls, but I don't think that taking an individual plant life compares to the violence of killing an animal."

The meat industry has been written about extensively in both fiction and nonfiction, for several reasons. First, animal-rights-activist authors believe strongly in their cause. And second, the subject is inherently dramatic, involving nothing less than life and death.

Alexander Cockburn writes about his observations when visiting a large slaughterhouse in Utah:

> They are using the captive bolt pistol within a steel box, and the back gate falls on the back of the animal, forcing it inside. It's a .22 caliber cartridge. The animal is thus stunned, then hoisted. The throat is cut, the knife is twisted up (the animal is upside down), and the heart is punctured.
>
> The conveyor belt goes very fast. The workers are on an elevated platform and each has a specific task. In one room, the workers are working with inhuman speed, manipulating the carcass, boring around the neck and vertebrae with a knife. I see a conveyor with hundreds of skinned heads, and another line of hundreds of hearts moving along at the same speed. Hearts that were beating only moments before.
>
> This is Dante's inferno: steam, noise, blood, smell, and speed. Sprinklers wash off meat; giant vacuum-packing machines use heat to seal twenty-two pieces of flesh a minute. Ground beef is packed into glycol and water, long sausage shapes trundle around to be laser scanned and packaged—ready to retail.

Both the beef and poultry industries have regulations designed to reduce animal pain and suffering as well as improve sanitation and safety. But in the real world, their recommendations are often ignored when the inspectors are not in the plant. One slaughterhouse worker comments:

Down in the blood pit they say the smell of blood makes you aggressive. And it does. You get an attitude that if that hog kicks at me, I'm going to get even. You're already going to kill the hog, but that's not enough. It has to suffer. A live hog would be running around the pit. It would just be looking up at me and I'd be sticking, and I would just take my knife and—eerk—cut its eye out while it was just sitting there. And this hog would just scream.

One time I took my knife—it's sharp enough—and I sliced off the end of a hog's nose, just like a piece of bologna. The hog went crazy for a few seconds. Then it just sat there looking kind of stupid. So I took a handful of salt brine and ground it into his nose. Now that hog really went nuts, pushing its nose all over the place. I still had a bunch of salt left on my hand—I was wearing a rubber glove— and I stuck the salt right up the hog's ass. The poor hog didn't know whether to shit or go blind.

It's not anything anyone should be proud of. It happened. It was my way of taking out frustration.

Although no one can deny there is something barbaric about killing animals for food, writer Barbara Holland makes the argument that, without the meat industry, these animals might not have a life at all:

All summer, the future hamburgers amble through the pleasant fields and wade in the pond. Stand together in the sprawling shade of the pasture tree. If you're walking by, they come to the fence. They like people. Big as a Buick, calm as a clam, the steer leans his chin on the top rail and asks to be rubbed right there....

Late in November, when you go by, the field is empty. But people like hamburgers, and if they didn't, the big sweet-smelling fellows, not being household pets, would never have lived at all to spend such a pleasant summer in such a green field.

The quality of life is not measured in years, and of course the steer has what Tennessee Williams called the pig's advantage: no premonition in the summer's field of the winter's Big Macs. Rather a pity we can't all buy into that, but worth keeping in mind.

Holland's logic aside, the meat industry can tolerate and even encourage extreme cruelty to animals, and its treatment of human workers is not much better:

According to the Occupational Safety and Health Administration (OSHA), meat, poultry, and fish-processing jobs are among the most hazardous in America. In 1990 the probability of incurring an injury in a meatpacking plant was three times higher than for manufacturing workers as a whole (U.S. Department of Labor, 1992).

A principal cause of excessive injury is the speed of the disassembly line along which carcasses are processed. Workers make thousands of repetitive motions each day, leading to cumulative trauma disorders, the most common being carpal tunnel syndrome.

Food-processing workers rarely earn a "living wage"—one sufficient for workers to maintain their households. The income needs for labor-force reproduction approximates federally established poverty levels, the income necessary to feed, clothe, and shelter a family of four.

Gross annual incomes from meatpacking jobs usually fall a few thousand dollars above or below these levels; income in poultry processing is less, while in fish processing earnings can fall to half of established poverty levels. These income estimates all assume workers will enjoy full employment, but seasonal slowdowns in demand, occasional plant closings, and occupational injuries reduce time on the job and hence reduce annual earnings.

When Upton Sinclair first published his classic novel about the Chicago stockyards, *The Jungle*, his goal was to help the poor immigrants who worked under near-slave conditions in the meat houses. We learned that the workers were taken advantage of by the meat companies, and that the animals often died inhumanely. But Sinclair also reported with great clarity and accuracy the unsanitary conditions under which the meat on America's dinner tables was produced. Here's one passage:

The beef had lain in vats full of chemicals, and men with great forks spread it out and dumped it into trucks, to be taken to the cooking room. When they had speared out all they could reach, they emptied the vat on the floor, and then with shovels scraped up the balance and dumped it into the truck.

This floor was filthy; yet they sent the "pickle" into a hole that connected with a sink, where it was caught and used over again forever; and if that were not enough, there was a trap in the pipe, where all the scraps of meat and odds and ends of refuse were caught, and every few days it was the old man's task to clean these out, and shovel their contents into one of the trucks with the rest of the meat.

And in 1850, the prestigious journal *Scientific American* gave this report of contamination in the sausage-making industry:

> German sausages are formed of blood, brains, liver, pork, flour, etc. and, with spice, are forced into an intestine, boiled and smoked. If smoking is not efficiently performed, the sausages ferment, grow soft and slightly pale in the middle; and in this state they cause, in the bodies of those who eat them, a series of remarkable changes followed by death.
>
> The poisonous power of fermenting sausages depends first on the atoms of their organic matter being in a state of chemical movement or transposition; and second that these moving molecules can impart their motion to the elements of the blood and tissues of those who eat them, a state of dissolution analogous to their own. Organic matter becomes innocuous when fermentation ceases; boiling, therefore, restores poisonous sausages, or being steeped in alcohol.

You might think tainted meat is a thing of the past. But you would be wrong. And a tiny bacteria is the culprit.

In January 1993, four children died and hundreds of people got sick after eating hamburgers tainted with this bacteria—*E. coli*—at Jack-in-the-Box restaurants in the Pacific Northwest.

In response, Jack-in-the-Box immediately established a comprehensive food-safety system, patterned after NASA's food-safety program for astronauts. They also worked with federal and state regulators, health officials, and consumer advocacy groups to bring about new laws and regulations.

Following the incident, Jack-in-the-Box posted strong earnings, and the communications team aggressively placed these positive business stories in the press, helping re-establish credibility as a viable company. Their parent company later reached a $58.5 million settlement with nine beef suppliers over the tainted burgers. The chain also made amends with victims' families.

In 1997, Hudson Foods recalled 25 million pounds of hamburger meat, and the earlier Jack-in-the-Box incident was again referenced in the media. At this point, the steps they had taken in 1993 helped them when the press started calling again.

Jack-in-the-Box's parent company, Foodmaker, positioned Dr. David Theno, the company's vice president of quality assurance, as an expert on *E. coli*. The public relations team developed press kits explaining that *E. coli* is a food-chain problem, not just a Jack-in-the-Box problem.

When you eat a steak, all the meat on your plate is from one animal, so the chances of your getting an animal that carried bacteria are small. But in both hot dogs and ground beef, you are eating meat from multiple animals, and so the odds of eating tainted flesh increase.

Because of this education program, the media in 1997 stated how far Jack-in-the-Box had come, how much they improved, and how much they recovered from the difficult situation in 1993. Public relations executive Eric Yaverbaum commented, "This case is an example of a company seeing a problem, taking steps to correct it (possibly above and beyond what other companies would do), and—because of these steps—being able to distance themselves when more outbreaks occurred and turn a bad situation into a positive one for the company."

Today *E. coli* contamination in beef remains a major threat to food safety. As Erich Schlosser explains in his best-seller *Fast Food Nation*:

E. coli 0157:H7 is a mutated version of a bacterium found abundantly in the human digestive system ... [it] can release a powerful toxin that attacks the lining of the intestine.

In about 4 percent of reported *E. coli* 0157:H7 cases, the toxins enter the bloodstream, causing hemolytic uremic syndrome (HUS), which can lead to kidney failure, anemia, internal bleeding, and the destruction of vital organs. The toxins can cause seizures, neurological damage, and strokes. About 5 percent of the children who develop HUS are killed by it. Those who survive are often left with permanent disabilities, such as blindness or brain damage.

Children under the age of five, the elderly, and people with impaired immune systems are the most likely to suffer from illnesses caused by *E. coli* 0157:H7. The pathogen is now the leading cause of kidney failure among children in the United States. Adults in perfect health can be stricken by the pathogen, too.

A recent USDA study found that during the winter about 1 percent of the cattle at feedlots carry *E. coli* 0157:H7 in their gut. The proportion rises to as much as 50 percent during the summer. Even if you assume that only 1 percent are infected, that means three or four cattle bearing the microbe are eviscerated at a large slaughterhouse every hour.

The odds of widespread contamination are raised exponentially when the meat is processed into ground beef. A single animal infected with *E. coli* 0157:H7 can contaminate 32,000 pounds of that ground beef. To make matters worse, the animals used to make about one-quarter of the nation's ground beef—worn-out dairy cattle—are the animals most likely to be diseased and riddled with antibiotic residues.

As Schlosser notes, the danger of contaminated beef is intensified when you eat "mixed meat"—hamburgers, hot dogs, canned meat, ground beef, and other meat made from multiple animals, rather than steaks, ribs, chops, and animal parts which naturally come from a single animal. In hot dogs and burgers, the meat from a single contaminated cow can be spread among dozens of patties or links.

In the case of *E. coli* contamination, hot dogs may actually be safer than burgers because of the way they are prepared. The spices used in smoking and curing are known to prevent the growth of certain microbes. Now scientists are finding spices helpful in killing *E. coli* in a variety of foods, including beef and chicken.

According to a study from Kansas State University, the equivalent of one tablespoon of prune puree per pound of hamburger can kill more than 90 percent of the *E. coli*. Acids in the prune juice do the trick.

Armour Swift-Ekrich, a major producer of processed meats, got the Agriculture Department's permission in 2000 to use higher amounts of sodium diacetate, a common meat flavoring, to prevent the growth of *Listeria monocytogenes*, another bacterial contaminant.

The bacterium can cause potentially fatal food poisoning that leads to meningitis. In addition, *Listeria* can cause listeriosis, a disease that sickens the elderly and pregnant women, but can also attack young people with weak immune systems.

Listeria bacteria are found in the guts of humans, birds, spiders, livestock, and other animals. The microbes thrive on refrigerated foods, such as meats in cold delicatessen display cases.

Antibiotics are used to control *Listeria*. Research has found that the herb ginkgo biloba may help kill *Listeria*.

Just because hot dogs contain microbe-killing spices does not mean they are exempt from contamination. In 1999, a man in upstate New York came down with flu-like symptoms after eating three Sabrett Skinless Beef Frankfurters for lunch. The next day, the federal government ordered a recall of 51,550 pounds of the meat—about 412,400 hot dogs—after finding them contaminated with bacteria.

In 2001, Sara Lee Corp. pleaded guilty to a misdemeanor and agreed to pay $4.4 million for selling tainted meat blamed for at least 15 deaths, 6 miscarriages, and 80 cases of serious illness in 1998. (There are 76 million cases of food-borne illness diagnosed in the United States each year, resulting in 5,000 deaths and 325,000 hospitalizations, according to the U.S. government.) The company's Bil Mar Foods division recalled 35 million pounds of hot dogs and lunch meat after its plant in Borculo, Michigan—about 20 miles west of Grand Rapids—was linked to an outbreak of listeriosis in December 1998.

Sara Lee was again plagued by meat contamination problems in January of 2000. When a child got sick shortly after eating a hot dog at a naval base in Norfolk, Virginia, the company voluntarily recalled 34,500 pounds of their Ball Park Franks hot dog packages.

The military sent four unopened packages of the hot dogs to its food-testing laboratory at Fort Sam Houston in Texas. Lab tests showed that one of the four packages contained *Listeria*, triggering the recall.

In food processing, food handling equipment is often fabricated of a high-grade stainless steel that resists contamination and is easy to clean. But new research from England's Center for Applied Microbiology and Research suggests that, for hot dog makers, copper might be a better choice. Their study suggests that *E. coli* bacteria are killed within hours of contacting copper surfaces.

Radiation may become the standard method of killing *E. coli* and other bacteria to prevent meat contamination. The Department of Agriculture's Food Safety and Inspection Service is proposing a maximum dose for irradiated fresh meat of 4.5 kilorads (450,000 rads)—less than one-tenth of the dose used by NASA to produce shelf-stable cooked meat for astronauts.

Donald Thayer, a microbiologist with the U.S. Department of Agriculture, says that one-third of the maximum proposed dose—1.5 kilorads—will eliminate 99.999 percent of *E. coli* organisms in beef.

Irradiation does not make beef radioactive; any more than having an x-ray makes you radioactive. There is some concern about radiation affecting the food chemically.

In meat, radiation has been shown to create such chemicals as benzene, a carcinogen. But, says Thayer, the chemical changes in irradiated meat at the proposed dosage levels are extremely small, in the parts per million or billion. So far studies show no evidence of ill effects from consuming irradiated meat.

Although irradiated beef is new, irradiated food is not. The FDA first approved food irradiation in the early 1960s, for insect control of wheat. In the 1980s, the FDA approved irradiated produce and spices, and in the 1990s, irradiated poultry.

While hot dogs may be safer than hamburgers from a bacterial contamination point of view, the news from the cancer front is not as favorable. A major ongoing study from the World Health Organization, tracking almost half a million people, shows that eating preserved red meats such as hot dogs—even just one hot dog a day—could increase the risk of bowel cancer by as much as 50 percent. So far, the study has not found a link between increased bowel cancer risk and eating fresh red meat, such as hamburger or steak.

If you like to grill your franks on the barbecue, the dangers are even greater. According to an article in *Science News*, grilling produces a type of carcinogen known as heterocyclic amines (HCAs). One method of preventing HCA formation on meat when grilling is to coat the hot dog in an antioxidant. Studies have found preliminary success with tart cherries, marinades, and vitamin E (you can add the contents of a 40 milligram vitamin E capsule).

This makes grilling tricky. HCA is not visible, and you can't detect it by smell or taste. A good rule of thumb is not to allow your hot dogs or other meat to become blackened. You can also pre-cook your meat in the microwave oven. The microwaving drives off some of the liquid, which may remove HCA's raw ingredients.

Recent research has identified other classes of carcinogenic compounds formed during grilling. Polynuclear aromatic hydrocarbons (PAHs) are formed when fat drips from the food onto the charcoal. The smoke rising up from the sizzling fat deposits PAHs on the surface of the meat.

Heterocyclic aromatic amines (HAAs) are created within muscle meats during cooking over hot coals. However, the risk of getting cancer from HAAs is very low—one in ten thousand over a lifetime.

And some good news: Drinking beer with your grilled dogs may be the best protective medicine of all. A study showed that stout ale can prevent HCA from forming adducts, which may be a first step on the path to many cancers.

If you have leftovers, how long can you keep them before they go bad? When uncooked hot dogs spoil, they have a foul odor—

you will know they are bad. They also form a layer of slime on the outside of the hot dog, which is repulsive to the touch.

Hot dogs should be refrigerated at 35 to 40 degrees Fahrenheit for no longer than four to five days. After that, throw them out. You can freeze hot dogs for up to a month.

Beef's woes are far from over. In addition to the threat of *E. coli*, a new illness, "Mad Cow Disease," appeared on the scene in the late 1990s. The scientific name is Creutzfeldt-Jakob Disease (CJD), also known as transmissible spongiform encephalopathies (TSEs) or bovine spongiform encephalopathy (BSE):

> On March 20, 1996, the news that ten young people had contracted CJD from eating infected beef shook England and all of Europe. Now ABC was reporting that undiagnosed cases of CJD could already be much more widespread in the United States than anyone had previously realized.
>
> "Health officials have maintained there are only about 250 new cases of CJD in this country each year, but several autopsy studies suggest this disease has been under-diagnosed," explained ABC's John McKenzie. "The studies show that when pathologists actually did autopsies and examined brain tissue from patients with Alzheimer's and other brain disorders, they uncovered hidden cases of CJD, anywhere from about 1 percent to 13 percent."
>
> These preliminary findings suggest a public health problem is being overlooked. If larger autopsy studies at more hospitals in this country confirmed that even 1 percent of Alzheimer's patients had CJD, that would mean 40,000 cases, and each undetected case is significant because, unlike Alzheimer's, CJD is infectious.

If the true number of CJD cases in the United States turns out to be 40,000 instead of 250, the implications for human health would be severe. It could mean that a deadly infectious dementia akin to Britain's problem has already entered the U.S. population.

And since CJD has an invisible latency period of up to 40 years in humans, 4,000 cases could be just the beginning of something much larger. Mad cow disease and CJD are related "transmissible spongiform encephalopathies" or TSEs. (The technical name for mad cow disease is "bovine spongiform encephalopathy" or BSE.)

What is particularly insidious about CJD is that it seems to be spread by the beef industry practice of feeding cows scraps of meat and organs from cows already slaughtered. Therefore one infected cow can be consumed by others, who are slaughtered and consumed by others, and so on in a vicious cycle. In other words, we sicken ourselves by forcing our farm animals to become cannibals—something the animal-rights activists might see as a case of what goes around, comes around.

Tips for Safe Handling of Hot Dogs and Other Meats

1. Buy meat from a refrigerated case. Keeping meat cold slows the growth of bacteria.

2. When at the supermarket, make meat the last thing you put in your cart (except for possibly ice cream) so it does not have time to reach room temperature before you get it home.

3. Keep your refrigerator no warmer than 40 degrees Fahrenheit.

4. After a backyard barbecue, don't leave the left-over hot dogs out for more than a couple of hours. Put them away in the refrigerator.

5. Store meat and poultry separate from fruits and vegetables, so juice dripping from meat or poultry (hot dog containers often drip juice when opened) won't contaminate your other food.

6. Wash your hands thoroughly before and after handling any meat, even sausage and hot dogs.

Chapter 6:

Hot Dogs and Nutrition

Samantha Heller, a senior clinical nutritionist at NYU Medical Center in New York City, recently criticized fictional detectives Briscoe and Green for eating hot dogs while working on cases on the TV show *Law and Order*. "We're talking high fat, high saturated fat, high sodium, and cancer-causing chemicals like nitrates," said Heller in an interview with the *New York Post*. "All told, hot dogs wreak havoc on the body."

Pediatrician M. Susan Jay disagrees. "Hot dogs are a source of protein which is necessary to maintain healthy bodily functions," says Dr. Jay. Should parents worry about the fat content in hot dogs?

"No," replies Jay. "As a pediatrician, I'm always reminding parents that most active kids shouldn't be cutting back on fat, because they'll get the calories and nutrients they need by balancing what they eat over time. Kids have different nutritional needs than adults, and putting them on diets may delay normal growth and development." For grown-ups with a weight problem, Jay recommends fat-free hot dogs.

My lifelong love of hot dogs falls under the category of "guilty pleasures." I feel guilty because I'm eating meat. And I feel guilty because when you eat a hot dog in public, people know what you're eating—and assume it's unhealthy. They can then form unseemly opinions about you, especially if you are a bit overweight, as I am. "He doesn't care about himself." "He's ignorant; doesn't he know how unhealthy that is?"

Are they right? One theory holds that the better something tastes, the worse it must be for you. You can perform this experiment at home for yourself. Put a piece of iceberg lettuce or celery on your tongue. Let your taste buds come in contact with it. Chew slowly and swallow. Now repeat with a piece of bacon. You see what I mean.

The hot dog, being extremely savory, would rank low on the nutritional scale based on this testing methodology. "The lowly hot dog is the most widely consumed sausage in the world," says chef Charles Revis. "It is also a nutritional nightmare. Fat, water, and salt make up more than fifty percent of the typical hot dog by weight. In addition to being nutritionally unsound, this makes the hot dog a very expensive source of protein.

"When all the other ingredients are factored in, the meat in a two-dollar-a-pound package of hot dogs is more costly than a pound of filet mignon at more than twice the cost." In many brands of hot dog, as much as 70 percent of the calories come from fat.

Cookbook author Mettja Roate takes the opposite stance. "Hail to the hot dog!" she writes. "Wieners are made from only the purest ground lean meat. It is wonderful protein food, equally good for young and old. Wieners contain the same top protein and meat value as very lean steaks and roasts. [They are] a truly time-saving, economical, delicious source of protein and energy for your family."

Many orthodox and alternative medical professionals now include hot dogs on their lists of allowable foods, even for patients on diets. The late Dr. Charles Atkins, for example, said it's okay to eat the hot dog, but you should avoid the bun (based on his theory that carbohydrates, not fat, cause illness and obesity).

What's in a Dog?

A 1.6-ounce hot dog contains approximately 5 to 7 grams of protein, 150 calories, 13 grams of fat, 30 milligrams of cholesterol, and 450 milligrams of sodium. A hot dog on a bun with relish has the same amount of protein, and no more calories, than an eight-ounce cup of low-fat flavored yogurt. A hot dog contains the same amount of protein as an egg, but with one-tenth the cholesterol.

Low-fat and reduced-fat hot dogs contain between one to nine grams of fat and 50 to 100 calories. Fat-free hot dogs have less than half a gram of fat and 35 to 40 calories. Approximately 41.7 million pounds of low-fat/no-fat hot dogs—representing 15 percent of total hot dog sales by volume—are sold annually. Hebrew National's Fat Free Beef Frank, for instance, has only 45 calories, 1.5 grams of fat, and 15 mg of cholesterol. The company advertises it as "97 percent fat free."

Chicken and turkey franks do not win the low-fat derby. Because the ground poultry they are made of contains a fair amount of dark as well as light meat, the fat content is fairly high. The Wampler Longacre Chicken Frank contains 11 grams of fat, 120 calories, and 480 milligrams of sodium. The Perdue Turkey Frank has 8 grams of fat, 100 calories, and 520 milligrams of sodium.

By comparison, Healthy Choice Low-Fat Beef Franks have only 1.5 grams of fat, 60 calories, 430 milligrams of sodium, and

15 milligrams of cholesterol. *Good Housekeeping* says this hot dog is "clearly the best balance between low fat and good taste."

Hot dog lovers skeptical of nutritional claims on labels can perform their own laboratory tests at home to determine fat content. Here's how:

Get four bowls. Pour half a cup of water into each. Label the bowls from left to right A, B, C, D. Add different amounts of sugar to each bowl as indicated in the table below and stir until the sugar dissolves.

Bowl	Amount of sugar in one cup of water (teaspoons)	Fat content of hot dog if it hovers	Fat content of hot dog if it sinks	Fat content of hot dog if it bobs
A	5	Less than 10%	Less than 10%	Over 10%
B	3 1/2	10 to 20%	Closer to 20%	Over 20%
C	2	20 to 30%	Closer to 30%	Over 30%
D	1	30 to 40%	Closer to 40%	Over 40%

Mash chunks of hot dog and put them in the bowls. Watch whether the meat hovers, sinks, or bobs. Then read the fat content from the table.

Despite the fat content, Weight Watchers includes hot dogs in its diet regimen. NASA approves hot dogs as part of the diet for astronauts on space missions.

U.S. Department of Agriculture requires hot dogs to be muscle meat, just like fresh ground beef sold in supermarkets.

Hot dogs include beef, water, salt, sugar, spices, and curing agents. Hot dogs can contain up to 3.5 percent non-meat ingredients including non-fat milk, cereal, or dried whole milk, or 2 percent isolated soy protein.

Organ meat if used must be indicated. The label would state "with variety meats" or "meat by-products."

All hot dogs are cured and pre-cooked, making them less susceptible to spoilage and contamination than other meat products. Sodium nitrate is used in the curing process. Other preservatives, such as hydrolyzed soy wheat and sodium erythrobate, may also be used.

Hot dogs contain, among other things, vitamin C, vitamin B, zinc, iron, protein, carbohydrates, riboflavin, niacin, and thiamin.

A Carnivore's Delight

My personal dilemma with loving hot dogs is the question of red meat, specifically whether to eat it and, if so, how much.

Aside from an increasing concern as I age with inhumane treatment to animals, I have a selfish concern centered around the link between red meat and such illnesses as high blood pressure, heart disease, and cancer.

One of the few clear-cut nutritional benefits of hot dogs is that they are high in protein. But does this offset the drawbacks? The fact is, you don't need to eat hot dogs to get protein; and you probably eat much more protein than you need from a variety of other sources. The average American diet contains more than twice the amount of protein the body needs, and the excess protein may be a precursor of cancer.

People who eat meat consistently have elevated rates of cancer. One major study published in the *British Medical Journal* involving 6,000 adults determined that meat eaters are twice as likely to die from cancer as vegetarians. After adjusting for non-dietary lifestyle factors, the vegetarian's risk of dying of cancer was still 40 percent less than that of the meat eaters!

These findings corroborate studies from Britain, Germany, Japan and Sweden, all showing that meat eaters suffer greater overall cancer deaths than do vegetarians.

Dr. T. C. Campbell's China Project shows that not just meat but all animal proteins have the potential to promote cancer, and Campbell cites other studies that show that carcinogenesis can be "turned on" by animal protein and "turned off" by plant protein.

"It appears that once the body has all the protein it needs—which it gets at only about 8-10 percent of the entire diet—than the excess protein begins to feed precancerous lesions and tumors," reports Campbell. "The average American diet contains more than twice the amount of protein than is needed, and much of it comes from meat, eggs, or dairy products."

And:

There is much evidence that the consumption of meat in the diet increases the probability of cancer of the large intestine. Vegetable fiber tends to absorb a variety of environmental pollutants and carry them out of the body. While eating bran could boost the fiber content of a meat-eater's diet, this is probably not an ideal solution.

Yet a meat diet is not necessarily unhealthy. When Weston Price traveled around the world, many of the groups he studied were very healthy despite eating diets partially or even totally made up of flesh foods. The ancient scriptures of India do not prohibit meat, but prescribe carefully which meats are most appropriate for which people. It is likely that many of the problems stemming from meat consumption today are due in part to the quality of the meat.

Even if one is comfortable with the idea of eating flesh foods, he will find that those available today are generally not wholesome. In the meat departments of many large supermarkets, sanitation is questionable, and much of the meat is contaminated or partly spoiled.

During the deterioration of the cells after death, bacterial growth begins. Meat's tendency to deteriorate causes significant hygienic problems during its packing and marketing which, unfortunately, have not been solved, even in the technologically advanced countries.

A great many samples of meat have been found to be infected with *Clostridium perfringens*. Toxins produced by this and other similar bacteria often found in meat are not destroyed by cooking—even though the bacteria are killed. Such toxins can cause serious gastrointestinal illness. When frankfurters from all over the United States were studied, over 40 percent had more than enough bacteria growing in them to consider them "spoiled" by accepted standards.

The conclusion: Yes, hot dogs are high in protein. But you don't have to depend on red meat to get your fill. Other sources are plentiful. They include meat, eggs, milk, cheese, beans, nuts, seeds, and grains.

One study reviewed people whose diets were based primarily on grains, vegetables, and beans, and who got less than 10 percent of their protein intake from meat, milk, and eggs. Even on these meat-poor diets, they were getting 50 percent more protein than required.

So cancer is one concern of the meat eater. Heart disease is another concern. Eating red meat is linked to cardiovascular illness, and the culprit is saturated fat.

"Saturated fats are solid at room temperature [and] are primarily found in animal products," explains Dr. Mitch Gaynor. "The liver uses saturated fat to manufacture cholesterol. Therefore, people who have high cholesterol levels will need to restrict their intake."

Americans eat an average of 10.6 ounces of red meat a day compared to 2.24 ounces daily for the Japanese. The average adult American male eats 30 percent more protein than he needs. "The problem with animal protein is that it is high in artery-clogging saturated fat and cholesterol," says Dr. David Ryback. "Besides that, most men eat more protein than they need, anyway."

Dr. Stephen Sinatra, a board-certified cardiologist, concurs: "The typical American diet is loaded with quantities of highly saturated fatty foods that overwhelm the vascular system. Thus, it is not surprising that Americans have a much higher incidence of heart disease than the Japanese or Mediterranean population, who tend to take in very little fat and whose diets are low in animal and dairy products." He points out that the African Bantu, whose diet is mostly beans, grains, vegetables, and fruit, have an average cholesterol level of only 90 to 100 mg/dl, and coronary heart disease is rare among the tribe.

The Chemicals in Hot Dogs

In the classic horror film *Motel Hell*, an innkeeper famed for his sausages and smoked meats keeps a gruesome secret: he makes them out of his guests! Solo travelers are captured, hog tied, and buried up to their necks in a field far from the main building. Their tongues are removed so they cannot scream. Then, like a cow, they are fattened up through force feeding until they are nice and plump and ready for slaughter. (One of these victims is played by John Ratzenberger, who later went on to fame as postal worker Cliff Claven in the NBC sitcom *Cheers.*)

The hero of the movie catches the innkeeper at his grisly work, where he chainsaws his victims' bodies in his basement while wearing a pig mask. They struggle, and the innkeeper falls onto the blade, receiving a fatal wound. As he dies, he confesses in the last line of the film: "My whole life was a lie—I used preservatives."

Hot dog makers use a number of food additives in their wieners. The most common is the preservative sodium nitrate.

Hot dogs are high in sodium, but not extraordinarily so when compared with other foods. An Oscar Mayer Big & Juicy deli-style beef frank has 920 milligrams of sodium, compared with 820 milligrams of sodium for a cheeseburger. A Louis Rich Bun-Length frank contains 870 milligrams of sodium vs. 400 milligrams in a serving of nachos with cheese sauce.

Also known as soda niter or Chile saltpeter, sodium nitrate is a colorless, odorless crystal that dissolves easily in water. It consists of one molecule of sodium, one molecule of nitrogen, and three molecules of oxygen. A related preservative, sodium nitrite, has a similar molecular composition except there are only two oxygen molecules instead of three.

Sodium nitrate is used as a preservative in many processed meats including hot dogs, salami, pepperoni, ham, bacon, and bologna. One reason is that sodium nitrate gives the meat a pink or reddish color that consumers favor. Without nitrate, the meat would look more brownish or grayish, liked cooked hamburger. Second, the nitrate inhibits the growth of botulism and other microorganisms.

There is no proven link between sodium nitrate and cancer, but there is enough evidence to make many consumers wary. Sodium nitrate reacts with acid and other chemicals in the stomach to produce nitrosamines, which have been shown to cause cancer in animals when consumed in large quantities. According to an article in *Health* magazine, nitrates can irritate nerve endings in the brain, causing migraine headaches.

However, the concentration of nitrates in cured meats has been greatly reduced in recent years, from 50 parts per million to about 10 parts per million. The U.S. Food and Drug Administration permits up to 200 parts per million of sodium nitrate in sausage. Cured meats such as hot dogs contain ascorbates, which prevent nitrates from forming nitrosamines.

Hot dogs often contain the chemical sodium erythrobate, also known as sodium isoascorbate. This is the ascorbate that prevents the nitrosamine-forming chemical reaction.

Sodium erythrobate is a white, odorless powder used as an antioxidant to add color and cure meat. Up to three quarters of an ounce of sodium erythrobate is added per 100 pounds of meat.

Both milk and soy proteins are used in hot dogs as filler or meat extenders. And some individuals are sensitive to soy, so check the label of your hot dogs before eating.

Soybeans contain trypsin inhibitors, hemagglutinins, saponins, estrogens, phystates, goitrogens, lysinoalanine, and other compounds known to cause adverse reactions in lab animals. The main effect is a build-up of gastrointestinal gas resulting in nausea, cramps, diarrhea, and flatulence.

Now, bad news for lactose-intolerant hot dog lovers: many hot dogs contain milk used as a binder. In fact, some hot dogs contain as much as 3.5 percent non-meat binders, such as nonfat dry milk, dried whole milk, 2 percent isolated soy protein, and cereal.

But the milk binder may be listed only as "flavoring," without identifying it as milk. Since kosher law does not allow meat and milk to be consumed together, kosher franks are milk-free and safe for the lactose-intolerant to digest.

Chapter 7:

Buns and Fixings

This chapter tells how hot dog buns evolved as hot dog vendors sought to shape bread dough to make the dogs easier to hold. It also covers the origins and varieties of mustard, horseradish, sauerkraut, relish, chopped onion, sauces, ketchup, chili, and other popular hot dog toppings—and why they are favored so much by hot dog lovers as condiments. The favorite hot dog topping is mustard, used by 87.6 percent of hot dog eaters.

Meat in Bread: An Idea Whose Time Has Come

Eating meat between bread is a fairly recent invention. John Montague, fourth Earl of Sandwich (1718-1792), is credited with inventing the sandwich. As the story goes, Montague liked to eat while he gambled. One day, he placed meat between two slices of bread so he could eat with one hand while he gambled with the other. This enabled him to eat without leaving the gaming table. When Captain James Cook discovered the Hawaiian Islands in 1778, he named them the Sandwich Islands in Montague's honor.

When did the hot dog become a sandwich? Some histories say a German immigrant sold hot dogs with sauerkraut on milk rolls from a pushcart on New York's Bowery during the 1860s.

Anton Feuchtwanger, a Bavarian concessionaire, was the first to serve hot dogs on special rolls—hot dog buns—made specifically for wieners. While serving hot dogs in 1904 at an exposition, he loaned his customers white gloves so they could hold the hot meat without burning their hands. When many of the gloves were not returned and the supply began to run low, Feuchtwanger asked his brother-in-law, a baker, for help. The brother-in-law baked special long soft rolls into which the hot dog neatly fit, inventing the hot dog bun.

Condiments

Although eating a hot dog plain can be pure joy, most people prefer their dogs with some sort of topping.

Rules of hot dog etiquette established by the National Hot Dog & Sausage Council list mustard, relish, onions, cheese, and chili as acceptable condiments. Ketchup is approved only for children age 18 and under. Fresh herbs are not on the approved list.

The Council also specifies the order in which condiments should be applied. First come wet condiments like mustard and chili. On top of that base, place the chunky condiments: relish, onions, sauerkraut, followed by shredded cheese. Last come spices such as celery salt or pepper.

The king of hot dog condiments may be Cousin Pete's, a lunch truck operating near Teterboro Airport in northern New Jersey. *The New York Times* called Pete's "the Baskin-Robbins of hot dogs."

They offer 52 varieties, all built using a variety of traditional and nontraditional toppings. The Elmer Fudd is topped with bacon bits and baked beans; the Dick Tracy, with hot peppers and potatoes.

"We had a customer who told us he used to eat peanut butter and banana sandwiches, and would we put it on a hot dog," says Greg Polandick, who owns Pete's with his wife Patty. "And he loved it. His name was Dan, and we said that's daring, so we named it the Daring Dan. And to be honest, it's very popular."

Mustard

Mustard is by far the most popular of the condiments served with hot dogs. A poll by Hebrew National says that 68 percent of hot dog eaters prefer mustard as their favorite condiment; a survey from the National Hot Dog and Sausage Council puts the figure at 87 percent. The New York Yankees have selected Gulden's—my personal favorite—as their "official" ballpark mustard.

All mustard is made in relatively the same way—from the crushed seeds of the mustard plant, the leaves of which are eaten as mustard greens. Indian mustard seeds, which are brown or black, are spicy. European and American mustard seeds are yellow or white, and milder. A few mustards, such as whole-grain mustard and *moutarde a l'ancienne,* are made from whole seeds.

Whether the hull and bran are sifted out during crushing depends on the type of mustard being made. The seed may go through further grinding and crushing.

A liquid—water, wine, vinegar, beer, citrus juices, or a combination of several of these liquids—is added, along with seasonings and other flavorings. The mustard is mixed, in some cases simmered, and then cooled. Some mustard is aged in large containers before it is bottled and shipped to stores and customers.

Although similar recipes for mustard paste appear as early as 42 A.D., the use of mustard as a condiment was not widely practiced in either Greece or Rome. Mustard seeds are, however, mentioned frequently in early Greek and Roman writings. Romans mixed the seeds with an unfermented grape juice they called *mustum ardens* (burning wine), from which we get the word mustard.

One anonymous ancient author said, "The distressed are quickly cured and the dead resuscitated, thanks to mustard!" Archaeologists have discovered mustard seeds packed in elaborate jars in tombs, an indication that they were used as a ritual offering to the gods in ancient times.

The ancient Egyptians ate the seeds whole. They took a bite of meat, dropped a few seeds into their mouth, and chewed meat and mustard seed together. Some scholars believe the popularity of mustard seed was due to its ability to mask the taste of spoiled meat.

The Romans took mustard seed to Gaul, and by the 9th century French monasteries were bringing in considerable income from mustard preparations. By the 13th century, mustard was one of the items offered by Parisian sauce-hawkers, who walked the streets at dinner peddling their savory wares.

For centuries, there was an increase in both the regulation of mustard and the number of makers. Contamination persisted until the middle of the 16th century, when regulations were instituted governing the cleanliness of all utensils used in production. In 1658, additional laws protected mustard producers, making it an offense for anyone else to make the sauce.

In spite of the wide acceptance of mustard and the regulations governing its production, its popularity declined by the early 18th century. The House of Maille, founded in 1747, was doing well in Paris, but general interest had ebbed, in part because of spices newly available from the Americas and the Far East. The market was revived, and the city of Dijon secured as the capital of mustard when, in 1856, Burgundian Jean Naigeon substituted verjuice for the vinegar in prepared mustard. The use of verjuice resulted in a mustard that was less acidic than France had tasted before, and the smooth, suave condiment we call Dijon assumed its place in history.

Although several mustard companies flourished in England, most notably Keen & Sons, founded in 1747, the English mustard producer to make an enduring name for himself did not come along until 1804. In that year, Jeremiah Colman, a miller of flour, began the first of several expansions that would make his name a synonym for mustard.

Today, Colman's mustard is prepared by much the same process that Jeremiah Colman developed. Two types of mustard seed—white and brown—are ground separately and sifted through silk cloth to separate the husks and the bran from the mustard flour. Originally, black mustard seed was used, but it was replaced by brown several decades ago. After grinding and sifting, the two mustards are mixed together and packaged in the famous yellow tins.

You can make your own mustard at home. Grind a half cup of mustard seed in a coffee grinder or blender until fine. In a double boiler, combine the ground mustard with a quarter cup of lemon juice, half a cup of water, and a pinch of salt and turmeric. Stir until smooth. Heat over simmering water, stirring frequently. Do not allow the mixture to come to a boil. Cool and thin as needed with extra water.

Like many foods with ancient roots, mustard has been used as a home remedy. Leaf mustard contains calcium, phosphorous, magnesium, and vitamin B. Mustard itself contains no cholesterol, only trace amounts of vegetable fat, and is composed of one-quarter to one-third protein. A gram of mustard flour contains only 4.3 calories.

Mustard stimulates appetite, aids digestion, and can help clear sinus passages. Mustard plaster has been used to treat wounds, since it increases blood flow to the inflamed areas of the body. Mustard flour sprinkled in socks is said to prevent frostbite of the toes. In 1982, John King applied for a U.S. patent to use mustard as an acne treatment. Five years earlier, William Vinson had applied for a U.S. patent to use mustard as a baldness cure.

Sauerkraut

If mustard is the number one hot dog topping, sauerkraut— essentially fermented cabbage—is surely right behind it.

Variations of fermented cabbage are eaten in many nations. When I visited Seoul, Korea, in the late 1970s, the first thing I noticed stepping off the plane was the pungent smell of kimche, a popular cabbage dish which people fermented in clay pots in front of their homes. When the fermenting mix is exposed to air, "kahm," a pasty white substance, forms on top of the contents. The kahm isn't harmful but must be removed since it gives the cabbage a bad taste. Every couple of weeks, the cloth, board, and stone that cover the cabbage in the crock are removed and washed.

Fermented cabbage was also eaten in China over 2,000 years ago by laborers as they built the Great Wall. One story has it that the poor workers building the wall owned no individual dishes, so all their cabbage and other vegetables were dumped into one crock. After a few days, the flavor started changing into something sharp and tasty.

Eventually, fermented cabbage became popular in Europe. Germans in particular liked the dish, naming it sauerkraut for "sour cabbage." In India, sauerkraut juice is made into a cabbage paste. The Russian version of sauerkraut, "kapusta," is a mixture of white cabbage, tomatoes, carrots, apples, pears, cucumbers, and herbs.

Modern sauerkraut, the kind you eat on hot dogs, is made by combining shredded cabbage, salt, and water, and allowing the mixture to ferment. Additional spices are optional.

Preparation is simple. You shred a pound of cabbage and put it in a stone crock or other container. Add 2 teaspoons of salt and mix thoroughly. Then pound the mixture with a mallet until you hear squishy sounds, meaning you are pounding hard enough to extract juice.

The extracted juice is what the cabbage ferments in. You can add water to make sure there is enough liquid to soak all the cabbage. Cover the mix with a few whole cabbage leaves. Spread a clean cloth over the top. Place a plate or board on the cloth to keep air from the mixture.

Put the crock in a warm spot. A temperature of 68 to 72 degrees is ideal. The cabbage takes two to six weeks to ferment into sauerkraut.

During fermentation, a scum forms on the surface of the brine, the cloth, and the board. Remove the scum from the surface daily by skimming it off, wash cloth and board in hot water, and then replace.

Sauerkraut is an excellent source of vitamins B and C. Father Kneipp, the German "father of natural healers," said about sauerkraut: "It is truly a broom for stomach and intestines. It takes away the bad juices and gases, strengthens the nerves and stimulates blood formation. You should eat it even if other cabbage is forbidden in your diet. Eat it moderately, well chewed, and do not drink anything with it."

Relish and Horseradish

Another popular hot dog condiment is relish. Relish is basically finely chopped vegetables with spices. Ingredients typically used in relish include hot peppers, zucchini, vinegar, sugar, salt, onions, scallions, cabbage, tomato, green pepper, carrots, and various spices.

To make your own onion relish, boil two to five unpeeled onions for five minutes, drain, and rub off the skins. Add one-third cup each of virgin olive oil and white wine vinegar; one and one-third cups of water; a teaspoon of sugar; and half a teaspoon of salt. Also add a chopped clove of garlic and half a teaspoon of mustard seeds. Season with half a teaspoon each of dry mustard and ground black pepper.

Mix and simmer until the onions are just tender. Stir in a third of a cup of raisins and simmer for three minutes more. Chill and serve.

Although usually coupled with roast beef sandwiches, horseradish is also served as a hot dog condiment. The plant is grown for its pungent roots, which contain an oil with a strong odor and hot, biting taste.

Horseradish can grow to a height of two to three feet when in flower. The tasty root grows entirely underground. The leaves and flower stalk are not eaten, nor does the plant usually produce seeds. To propagate the plants, pieces of side root are cut from the main root during harvest and replanted in the soil.

Horseradish sauce can be made by mixing grated horseradish with lemon juice, vinegar, sugar, and mustard. It should be chilled prior to serving.

Chili

Texans have been eating chili for over a century; some say since as far back as the 18th century. In 1977, chili became the state dish of Texas.

Chili scholar Everett DeGolyer wrote that chili had its origins in a dish called "pemmican of the Southwest." Pemmican was made of jerky, fat, and native chili peppers pounded together to form a concentrated and nutritious nonperishable trail ration. The dish is mentioned in the journal of George Evans, who journeyed to California in search of gold in the 1800s.

The Spaniards who came to America 300 years earlier found the Plains Indians cooking a similar dish. The Native Americans cut buffalo, venison, or beef into thin slices, dried it in the sun, and ground it into a powder. They mixed it in a pot with chilipiquin, a hot wild pepper.

Chili is a mixture typically made of beef and beans seasoned with chili peppers, somewhat thicker and much hotter than stew. During the Great Depression, chili was widely available at lunch counters because it was cheap and substantial. During World War II, as meat and spice were rationed, people ate chili less frequently.

In the 1960s, chili became popular again, perhaps because President Lyndon Johnson was a chili fan (in much the same way that Franklin Delano Roosevelt's fondness for hot dogs had helped make them popular decades earlier). He often had it served at the White House and always stocked it on Air Force One.

"Texas red chili can only truly be Texas red if it walks the thin line just this side of indigestibility: damning the mouth that eats it and defying the stomach to digest it, the ingredients are hardly willing to lie in the same pot together," says John Thorne, editor of *Simple Cooking*.

One recipe for "Texas Red" chili con carne is as follows:

> Put 3 pounds of beef chuck, with the fat trimmed, through the coarse blade of a meat grinder. Brown in small batches in bacon fat in a large skillet over moderately high heat. Transfer the cooked meat to a second large heavy skillet using a slotted spoon. Set aside. Wash 6 dried ancho peppers in cold water. Discard the stems and seeds. Tear the peppers into 2-inch pieces. Place the pieces in a small saucepan with cold water. Cover and simmer for 20 minutes.
>
> Drain, reserving the cooking water. Peel the skin from the peppers. Place in the work bowl of a food processor. Add the reserved water. Puree with short pulses. Mix the pepper puree into the beef. Add water; bring to a boil over high heat. Reduce heat to a slow simmer. Cover and simmer for 30 minutes.
>
> Stir in oregano, crushed cumin seeds, salt, cayenne, and crushed garlic. Cover and simmer for 45 minutes. Mix in 2 tablespoons of Mexican hominy flour. Cover. Reduce heat to the lowest possible. Cook 30 minutes longer, stirring occasionally so the mixture doesn't stick. If too thick, thin with small amounts of boiling water. Serve.

Pepper has several interesting properties, not all of them wholly desirable. For one thing, it may be addictive, like nicotine or cocaine. Numerous pepper eaters admit to getting high or experiencing a subtle euphoria from eating pepper.

Many people believe pepper to be a sexual stimulant. In 1970, following an outbreak of sexual offenses in prisons, the Peruvian government banned the serving of hot pepper sauces in prison cafeterias, claiming that they aroused sexual desires and were therefore inappropriate fare. The Turks used crushed red peppers in love potions.

Brahmacharya, the principles for attainment of purity of soul and body, forbid India's young Brahmans from eating hot peppers. The peppers were believed to produce too much heat in the body system, making blood and sexual fluids watery and the mind restless.

David Livingstone, of Stanley and Livingstone fame, reported that native African women bathed in water spiced with dissolved pepper juice to make themselves more attractive to the opposite sex. In medieval India, pepper was used as an aid in bringing women to orgasm.

Peppers contain an odorless, tasteless substance called capsaicin, which has been used as a pain killer to treat arthritis and other ailments. Clinical studies have shown that as many as 80% of arthritis sufferers experienced significant pain relief with topical capsaicin. Pain relief occurs almost immediately after the cream is applied to the afflicted area.

Published research indicates that the therapeutic benefit of capsaicin may be related to the reduction of inflammatory mediators in the synovial fluid of arthritic joints. By decreasing the activity of sensory neurons, the capsaicin produces analgesia (absence of sensitivity to pain).

Ketchup

The Hebrew National survey mentioned earlier in this chapter says that 47 percent of hot dog eaters use ketchup as their condiment. Kids are the biggest lovers of ketchup on hot dogs; a lot of adults say "yuck" when I mention it. When I was a child in the 1960s, hot dogs with ketchup were a favorite served by our counselors at camp. We called the concoction "Laddy Boys."

Purists are firmly against Laddy Boys. "Look at the hot dog as a wurst," says Barry Levenson, founder of the Mount Horeb Mustard Museum in Wisconsin. "In Europe, on the streets of Frankfurt or Vienna, they would never think of putting ketchup on a wurst. It doesn't challenge the sausage. You need an aggressive flavor. Would you put ketchup on a pastrami sandwich?"

Contrary to popular belief, ketchup was not invented in the United States. The earliest ketchup recipes were, according to culinary historian Andrew Smith, published in Great Britain in the 18th century. And the ketchup was not just made from tomatoes; kidney beans, mushrooms, anchovies, and walnuts were also used as a base ingredient.

One of the first tomato-based ketchups to be marketed commercially was made by Bunker and Company in New York City in 1834. Heinz began its operation in 1869, and patented its ketchup bottle—with its trademark keystone label, neck band, screw cap, and octagonal-shape—in 1882. In the early 1900s, Heinz became the largest tomato ketchup producer with the biggest canning factory in the world.

"Everybody loves ketchup," says Bill Johnson, CEO of Heinz. "We sell more than $1 billion worth in 140 countries. In the U.S., nine out of ten homes have ketchup."

The following recipe for home-made ketchup appears in a popular cookbook published in 1871:

1 peck ripe tomatoes
1 ounce salt
1 ounce mace
1 tablespoonful black pepper

1 teaspoonful cayenne
1 tablespoonful cloves (powdered)
7 tablespoonfuls ground mustard
1 tablespoonful celery seed (tied in a thin muslin bag).

Cut a slit in the tomatoes, put into a bell-metal or porcelain kettle, and boil until the juice is all extracted and the pulp dissolved. Strain and press through a colander, then through a hair sieve. Return to the fire, add the seasoning, and boil at least five hours, stirring constantly for the last hour, and frequently throughout the time it is on the fire. Let it stand twelve hours in a stone jar on the cellar floor. When cold, add a pint of strong vinegar. Take out the bag of celery seeds and bottle, sealing the corks. Keep in a dark, cool place.

Chapter 8

Favorite Hot Dog Recipes

Nutritional concerns aside, hot dogs are an ideal food for many reasons. Aside from low cost, dishes in which hot dogs are the main ingredient are almost impossible to screw up: Since hot dogs are a precooked food, there's little danger of under- or over-cooking. (See chapter 9 for cooking guidelines). And their spicy flavor ensures that dishes in which they are used won't be bland.

Hot dogs fit in well with the busy lifestyle of today's consumer. They can be cooked in a few minutes, and no marinating or other special preparation is required. "Except for canned meats, frankfurters are the most readily available and easiest to prepare of meats," says food expert James Beard. "They are cheap, nourishing, and quickly prepared, and with a little ingenuity you can make a pound of them serve four."

Purists may eat their dogs on a bun with or without toppings, but my favorite hot dog dish is the old standby, franks and beans:

Franks n' Beans
2-3 hot dogs
1 can baked beans (any major brand)
Mustard

Cut the hot dogs at an angle into quarter-inch pieces. Empty can of baked beans into pot and add hot dog pieces. Cook on low heat, stirring occasionally, until the liquid from the beans is simmering and the hot dog pieces are hot. Stir in a little spicy deli mustard and serve.

Canned baked beans make a perfect franks-and-beans meal. Almost all of the major brands are tasty, but I have a preference for B&M and Heinz. Half a century ago, cookbook author Hermay Smith gave the following recipe for home-made "Michigan baked beans":

1 quart peas or navy beans
½ pound lean bacon, cut in half-inch cubes
1 large onion, diced
½ teaspoon thyme
1 teaspoon dry mustard
2 teaspoons salt
6 tablespoons brown sugar
Boiling water

Soak the beans overnight in cold water to cover, with one-half teaspoon soda. Drain. Cover with fresh water and cook slowly from forty to sixty minutes, or until the skins pop when beans are taken up and blown on. Fry the bacon cubes until the edges begin to brown; remove, and in the fat cook the onion till slightly browned.

Put the beans in the pot, sprinkling each layer with the bacon cubes, onion, and thyme. Mix the brown sugar, salt, and mustard; add one cup boiling water, mix well, and pour over the beans, adding enough boiling water to cover. Bake covered at 250 to 300 degrees F. for six to eight hours. Add water if needed to keep the beans covered. Bake uncovered the last half hour to brown.

Two other ways to enjoy your hot dogs are to cut them up into quarter-inch slices, cook, and add to either macaroni and cheese or split pea soup. Sheer heaven!

Of course, professional cookbook authors have created recipes way more creative than just slice-and-heat. Here is a collection of the tastiest as well as the most unusual recipes I have found.

Chili Dogs

4 hot dogs
4 buns
1 tablespoon softened butter
1 large onion
1-2 garlic cloves
1 red chili pepper
¼ pound mushrooms
1 tablespoon oil
1 tablespoon tomato paste
½ cup cheddar cheese, grated

Peel and thinly slice the onion. Peel and crush the garlic. Cut the chili pepper along its length and remove the seeds and membrane. Clean mushrooms and slice thinly.

Heat the oil in a skillet, then gently cook the onion, garlic, and chili pepper for 4-8 minutes or until softened. Stir frequently during cooking. Add the mushrooms and continue to cook for 2 minutes. Blend the tomato paste with one tablespoon of water, then stir into the pan and cook for 3 minutes.

Place the hot dogs in a pan and cover with water. Cook over gentle heat for 5 minutes. Split the buns and spread with softened butter. Place the hot dogs in the rolls and top with the chili topping.
Serves 4

Crunch Beans and Wiener Casserole

1 can (1 lb. 5 oz.) Van Camp's pork and beans
½ lb. wieners, sliced
2 tablespoons molasses
2 tablespoons ketchup
1 can (3 oz.) French fried onion rings

Combine first four ingredients in greased 1 ½ quart casserole. Bake uncovered at 350° F for 30 minutes. Top with onion rings and bake an additional 30 minutes.
Serves 6

Frankly Mexican Casserole

1 package French's scalloped potatoes
½ pound frankfurters, sliced
1 can (15 oz.) kidney beans, drained and rinsed
1 tablespoon butter or margarine
¼ cup fine dry bread crumbs
½ teaspoon chili powder

Prepare potatoes as directed on the package, except use 2-quart casserole and increase boiling water to 2 cups. Stir in frankfurters and beans. Bake in 400° F oven 35 minutes; stir casserole. Melt butter in small pan; stir in bread crumbs and chili powder. Sprinkle over casserole and bake 10 to 15 minutes longer, until potatoes are tender.

Serves 6

Franks n' Crescents

8 frankfurters, partially split
Cheddar cheese cut into strips
1 8-oz. can Pillsbury refrigerated quick crescent dinner rolls

Heat oven to 375° F. Fill each frankfurter with strips of cheese. Separate crescent dough into 8 triangles. Place frankfurter on wide end of triangle and roll up. Place on greased cookie sheet, cheese side up. Bake at 375 degrees Fahrenheit 10 to 12 minutes or until rolls are golden brown.

Serves 8

Fruit Dogs

4 hot dogs
4 buns
1 satsuma
1 cup seedless grapes
1 kiwi fruit
2 teaspoons softened butter
2 celery sticks
½ cup walnuts or pecans
1 apple
1 tablespoon lemon juice
1 pound blue cheese
1 cup mayonnaise

Trim, wash, and dice celery. Chop nuts finely. Place celery and nuts in a bowl. Cut apple into pieces and sprinkle with lemon juice. Add the apple to the celery and nuts, and mix. Crumble blue cheese into mixture and add mayonnaise. Mix lightly. This makes a blue cheese relish that will keep for 2-3 days in the refrigerator if covered.

Peel the satsuma and divide into segments, discarding as much of the pith as possible. Cut segments in half and place in a clean bowl. Rinse grapes, cut in half, and add to bowl. Peel the kiwi, chop into small pieces, add to the other fruit, and mix lightly.

Split the buns and spread with softened butter. Place the hot dogs in a pan and cover with water. Cook over gentle heat for 5 minutes. Put fruit mixture on the split buns and top with the cooked hot dog. Spoon on a little blue cheese relish and serve.

Serves 4

Hot Dog and Macaroni Casserole

7-ounce package macaroni (2 cups uncooked)
½ cup onion, chopped
¼ cup green pepper, cut
2 tablespoons butter or margarine
2 tablespoons flour
1½ cup milk
1 cup carrots, grated
½ cup sour cream
½ teaspoon salt
¼ teaspoon dill weed
10 frankfurters, split lengthwise

Prepare macaroni according to package directions. Drain. Sauté onion and green pepper in butter until tender. Add flour and cook, stirring constantly for 2 minutes. Do not brown. Stir in milk and cook until smooth and thickened.

Remove from heat. Add macaroni, carrots, sour cream, salt, and dill weed. Arrange frankfurters vertically around a deep 1½-quart casserole. Pour macaroni mixture in center. Bake at 350° F for 25—30 minutes.

Serves 6

Hot Dogs and Onions

Pat of butter or margarine
1 package hot dogs
2 jumbo onions

Cut hot dogs into slices. Melt butter in large fry pan. Cut up onions and sauté in butter 10 minutes or less. Add hot dog slices and mix. Cover and heat until hot. Serve on hot dog buns or bread.

Serves 4

Microwave Hot Dogs

4 hot dogs
butter
4 hot dog buns
2 large onions
oil
caster sugar

Peel and slice onions. Push the onion slices through to form rings.

Heat the oil for 2 to 3 minutes in the microwave, in a large bowl, at full power. Toss in the onions so they are well coated in the oil. Cover and heat for 5 minutes. Stir well and dust with a little caster sugar. Cover and cook for 3-4 minutes until tender.

Heat frankfurters for 1-1½ minutes. Cut rolls down one side and spread with butter. Place onions and hot dogs inside rolls and reheat for 1-1½ minutes.

Serves 4

Split-Pea Soup with Hot Dogs

2–3 hot dogs
1½ cups lentils or green split peas
8 cups stock
1 large onion stuck with 2 cloves
1 bay leaf
2 cloves garlic
Salt, freshly ground pepper, to taste
Crisp fried croutons

Soak the split peas overnight, unless they are the quick-cooking variety. Wash them and add to the stock with the onion, bay leaf and garlic. Add two to three sliced-up hot dogs.

Bring to a boil, skim off any scum, reduce the heat and simmer until the peas or lentils are thoroughly cooked. Remove the bay leaf and onion and taste for seasoning. Serve the soup as it is, or puree it. Top with the croutons.

Frankfurter Frittata

6 tablespoons butter
1 medium onion, thinly sliced
½ green pepper, chopped fine
4 to 5 frankfurters, cut in shreds
6 eggs, beaten

½ cup grated Parmesan cheese
¼ cup chopped parsley
1 teaspoon salt
¼ teaspoon Tabasco

Melt the butter in a skillet and cook the onion and green pepper until the onions are just golden. Add the frankfurters and cook until delicately browned and cooked through—about 5 minutes. Pour over them the eggs mixed with the cheese, parsley and seasonings and cook until eggs are just set. Put under the broiler for 3 to 4 minutes to brown the top a little. Serve cut into wedges with potato salad or coleslaw.

Serves 4

Frankfurters in Sour Cream

1 pound (about 8) frankfurters
3 tablespoons butter
1 small onion, chopped
1 cup chili sauce or ketchup
1 cup heavy cream, sour cream or evaporated milk
Beurre Manie
Salt, freshly ground pepper to taste

Cut the frankfurters into long shreds. Melt the butter in a skillet, add and lightly brown the onion, then add the frankfurter shreds and toss them around until they are heated through. Then add chili sauce or ketchup and let it come to a boil. Stir in the cream, sour cream or evaporated milk and blend until smooth. Thicken, if you wish, with Beurre Manie. Simmer until thickened, correct seasoning and serve with rice or noodles or on toast.

Serves 4

Sweet and Sour Frankfurters

1 pound frankfurters, cut into 2-inch lengths
4 tablespoons oil
1 onion, cut rather coarsely
1 green pepper, seeded and shredded
1 cup pineapple chunks with juice
2 small tomatoes, peeled, seeded and quartered
2 tablespoons cornstarch
¼ cup white wine or dry vermouth
2 tablespoons white wine vinegar

Steam the frankfurters for 10 minutes in a little salted boiling water. Keep warm.

Meanwhile, heat the oil in a large skillet and add the onion, green pepper, pineapple chunks and juice and tomatoes. Cook just until well blended and heated through. Mix the cornstarch with a little water to make a paste and stir into the skillet with the vinegar and wine. Stir until smooth and thickened. Mix in the drained frankfurters and simmer 5 minutes.

Serve with steamed rice. Serves 4

Frankfurters in Spaghetti Sauce

1 large onion, chopped
1 clove garlic, chopped
4 tablespoons oil
1 twenty-nine-ounce can (3½ cups) Italian tomatoes
Basil or thyme
1 teaspoon sugar
6 frankfurters, finely ground
Salt, freshly ground pepper
½ cup chili sauce or ketchup

Sauté the onion and garlic in the oil. Add the tomatoes, a pinch of basil or thyme and the sugar. Bring to a boil, reduce heat and simmer uncovered for 25 minutes. After the sauce has cooked for 15 minutes, add the ground frankfurters, salt and pepper to taste and the chili sauce or ketchup.

Serve with spaghetti or noodles and grated Parmesan cheese. Serves 4

Turkish Frankfurters

1 large onion, coarsely chopped
1 or 2 cloves garlic, chopped
4 or 5 tablespoons oil
1 medium eggplant, peeled, dried and floured
Salt, freshly ground black pepper to taste
Thyme or basil
1 twenty-ounce can (2½ cups) tomatoes
1 pound frankfurters, cut into 1-inch pieces

Sauté the onion and garlic in the oil until golden and limp. Add the eggplant, salt and pepper to taste and a pinch of thyme or basil. Toss lightly until eggplant is browned. Add the tomatoes and allow them to cook down well. Add the frankfurters and simmer 20 minutes.

Serve with rice. Serves 4

Tasty Frankfurter Sandwich Filling

¾ cup (½ pound) processed American cheese, grated
3 tablespoons milk
3 frankfurters, chopped
1 tablespoon prepared mustard

Combine cheese and milk in top of a double boiler, when cheese has melted, add chopped frankfurters and mustard; mix well. Makes approximately 1 cup, or filling for 5 sandwiches.

Frankfurters with Fruit Sauce

1 pound frankfurters
1 can apricots, about 1 cup
1 tablespoon Worcestershire sauce
2 level tablespoons soft brown sugar
4 tablespoons vinegar
Salt and pepper
Hot dog rolls for serving

Separate frankfurters. Drain apricots, but reserve the syrup. Press fruit through a sieve or puree in a food processor or electric blender. Add Worcestershire sauce, sugar, vinegar, and salt and pepper to the apricots, with enough of the syrup to make a thick pouring sauce. Heat gently, stirring until simmering.

Cook frankfurters over a hot fire, basting with sauce. Turn and baste frequently until hot (about 5 minutes). Put each frankfurter in a roll. Heat remaining sauce and spoon over frankfurters before serving.

Makes 4 to 6 servings.

Cheese-Stuffed Frankfurters

1 pound frankfurters (8 to 10)
OPEN PIT ® Barbecue Sauce
2 to 3 slices processed American cheese, cut in thin strips
8 to 10 bacon slices
8 to 10 frankfurter rolls, toasted

Slit frankfurters lengthwise to ¾-inch from each end. Spoon ¼ teaspoon barbecue sauce along slit in each; add 2 cheese strips to each. Wind a bacon slice around each frankfurter; secure with wooden picks at each end. Place on grill, away from glowing coals. Brush with additional barbecue sauce and grill, turning and basting until bacon is cooked. Remove picks.

Serve on rolls. Makes 4 servings.

Sloppy Dogs

1 pound ground beef
1 package (1.5-oz.) DURKEE Sloppy Joe Seasoning Mix
1 can (6-oz.) tomato paste
1¼ cups water
1 teaspoon DURKEE Dry Mustard
2 teaspoons DURKEE Red-hot! Sauce
1 package (16-oz.) frankfurters
8-10 hot dog buns

In a 2½-quart casserole, crumble beef. Microwave on high 4-5 minutes, stirring halfway through cooking time; drain. Stir in seasoning mix, tomato paste and water. Microwave covered on high for 4 minutes. Stir halfway though cooking time. Add mustard, hot sauce, and frankfurters. Microwave covered on high for 6 minutes, stirring halfway through the cooking time.

Serve on hot dog buns. Makes 8 to 10 servings.

Taco Dogs

8 PERDUE® Franks
8 taco shells
15-ounce can chili with beans

1 cup shredded Monterey Jack or Cheddar cheese
Taco sauce
1 cup shredded lettuce
½ cup diced tomato

Preheat oven to 350°. Split franks in half lengthwise and grill or fry briefly. Place franks in taco shell and top each with 2 tablespoons chili and 1 tablespoon cheese. Place tacos on baking sheet and bake at 350° for 15 minutes, or until chili is hot and cheese is melted. Top with taco sauce, lettuce, tomato and remaining cheese. Serve immediately.

Serves 6-8

Hot dogs AZTECA®

1 pkg. AZTECA® flour or corn tortillas
1 lb. hot dogs
1 (15-oz.) can of chili with beans
1 (8-oz.) pkg. American cheese slices

Bring AZTECA® tortillas to room temperature. Preheat oven to 475°. Spread 1 heaping teaspoon of chili on each tortilla. Place slice of cheese on top of chili. Set hot dog in center of cheese. Roll up sides of tortilla and fasten with toothpicks. Bake approximately 10 minutes until cheese is melted and tortilla is crisp.

Serves 5-6

For appetizers, slice in quarters.

Croissant Dogs

8 PERDUE® Franks
8-ounce package of crescent roll dough

2 tablespoons Dijon mustard
2 slices Swiss cheese, 7 x 4 inches
1 egg beaten with 1 tablespoon water
1½ teaspoons poppy seeds (optional)

Preheat oven to 375°. Pierce franks all over with tines of fork. Divide crescent rolls and place on lightly floured surface. Working with one piece of dough at a time, fold tips of long side of triangle in to meet at center. Then stretch triangle lightly up toward point.

Cut cheese slices in half, then diagonally to form four triangular pieces. Brush dough with thin layer of mustard, top with cheese, brush with mustard again. Roll franks in the dough, starting at the bottom and rolling toward the point.

Place on ungreased baking sheet so they are not touching. Brush lightly with egg wash and sprinkle with poppy seeds. Place in the middle of the oven for 15 to 20 minutes or until dough is golden brown.

Serves 6-8

Hot Dog-Mushroom Rarebit

2–3 hot dogs
1 (10½ ounce) can condensed cream of mushroom soup
1 (3-ounce) can sliced mushrooms, drained
½ cup milk
4 slices American cheese, shredded
½ teaspoon prepared mustard
Paprika
4 slices Italian bread, toasted

Blend soup and milk in the top of a double boiler, over a low flame. Add cheese, mushrooms and mustard and place the pan over hot water. Stir and heat until cheese melts. Add the hot dogs, cut into ½-inch slices, and heat thoroughly. Pour over toast. Sprinkle with paprika. For buffet suppers, the rarebit may be kept warm in a covered chafing dish.

Serves 4

Westchester Hot Dog Salad

2 hot dogs
½ pound macaroni, uncooked
1 (8-ounce) can spaghetti sauce
8 ribs celery, sliced thin
10 radishes, sliced thin
½ cup sweet pickle, diced
2 hard-boiled eggs, chopped
¾ cup mayonnaise
¼ cup evaporated milk
1 tablespoon pickle juice
2 tablespoons prepared mustard
1 tablespoon instant minced onion
Salt and pepper to taste
2 tomatoes, cut into quarters
Paprika

Cook the macaroni according to the package directions. Drain, rinse with cold water and drain again. Sprinkle with the spaghetti sauce. Add all the other ingredients except the tomatoes, hot dogs and paprika. Place in a large bowl and chill.

Arrange tomato wedges around edges of bowl. Sprinkle hot dogs, cut into ½-inch slices, on top of all. Sprinkle paprika on top of hot dogs.

Serves 8

Hot Dogs Amandine

8 hot dogs
4 ribs celery, diced
2 tablespoons cooking oil
1 (1-pound) can pineapple chunks
¾ cup water
1 tablespoon soy sauce
1½ tablespoons vinegar
2 tablespoons cornstarch
1 teaspoon ginger
½ teaspoon garlic salt
½ teaspoon monosodium glutamate
1 green pepper, cut into 1 inch squares
¼ cup almonds, slivered

Sauté the hot dogs, cut diagonally into thirds, and celery in the cooking oil. Drain pineapple chunks. Combine the pineapple juice with water, soy sauce and vinegar. Mix together the cornstarch, garlic salt and monosodium glutamate. Add pineapple juice mixture to the dry ingredients, and stir until free of lumps. Pour the pineapple juice combination over the hot dogs and celery.

Stirring constantly, cook until thickened and clear. Add pineapple chunks and green pepper squares. Allow to simmer gently until pineapple chunks and pepper squares are hot. Sprinkle with almond slivers before serving.

Serves 4

Florentine Hot Dog Loaf

8 hot dogs
2 cups cooked spinach, chopped and drained

2 cups cooked rice
1 can condensed cheese soup
2 tablespoons milk
½ cup American cheese, grated
4 teaspoons parsley, chopped

Preheat the oven to 375°. Arrange the spinach evenly over the bottom of a loaf-shaped, buttered baking dish. In a separate bowl, combine the rice, soup and milk. Spread this mixture evenly over the spinach. Arrange the hot dogs on top. Bake for 20 minutes. Sprinkle the grated cheese over the hot dogs and bake for an additional 5 minutes, or until the cheese is melted. Remove from the oven. Sprinkle the chopped parsley over the hot dogs. Serve in the baking dish.

Serves 4 to 5

Hot Dogs Risotto

12 hot dogs
1½ cup rice
1½ cup water
½ teaspoon salt
2 teaspoons prepared mustard
1 can condensed cream of mushroom soup
¼ cup parsley, chopped
1 small onion, minced
2 tablespoons pimiento, chopped
1 cup Cheddar cheese, grated

Combine the rice, water and salt in a saucepan and bring quickly to a boil. Remove from heat, fluff the rice with a fork.

Cover quickly and allow to stand for 5 minutes. Combine rice with the soup, parsley, onion and pimiento. Slit the hot dogs lengthwise, but not completely through, to form "pockets." Stuff with the rice mixture. Sprinkle with grated cheese and bake in a 350° oven for 20 minutes.

Serves 6

Hot Dog Flambé

10 hot dogs
¼ cup granulated brown sugar
¼ cup cornstarch
¼ cup vinegar
¼ cup orange marmalade
1 cup pineapple juice
1 (13-ounce) can pineapple tidbits, with juice
½ cup seeded and split green grapes
10 Maraschino cherries
1 cup drained Mandarin orange sections
½ cup Cointreau

Mix together the granulated brown sugar and the cornstarch. Set aside. Mix together the vinegar, orange marmalade, pineapple juice and undrained pineapple tidbits in a chafing dish. Stir in the sugar cornstarch mixture, and continue to stir while heating until thickened. Add the hot dogs, cut diagonally into quarters, grapes, cherries and orange sections. Bring the chafing dish to the table, along with the Cointreau. Continue to heat. Pour the Cointreau over all. Ignite and serve with a flourish.

Serves 6

Hot Dog Stuffed Cabbage

4 hot dogs
4 outer leaves from a cabbage
½ cup crumbled corn flakes
½ small onion, minced
¼ teaspoon celery seeds
Salt and pepper, to taste
2 teaspoons sugar
½ teaspoon Worcestershire sauce
1 egg, well-beaten
1 tablespoon butter or margarine, melted
1 (1-pound) can solid packed tomatoes
¼ cup Cheddar cheese, grated

Mince 4 hot dogs. Simmer the cabbage leaves in water in a covered pot for 5 minutes; drain and spread out for filling. Combine the minced hot dogs with the crumbled corn flakes, onion, celery seeds and salt and pepper. Spoon one-fourth of this mixture onto the center of each cabbage leaf. Roll up each cabbage leaf, folding the ends toward the center. Secure the ends with toothpicks.

Curried Hot Dogs

4 hot dogs
2 small onions, chopped
1 cored apple, chopped
3 tablespoons butter or margarine, melted
1 tablespoon curry powder
1 tablespoon flour
1 cup boiling water
2 bouillon cubes

Sauté the onions, apple and hot dogs, cut crosswise into 1-inch slices, in the butter until onions are transparent. Dissolve bouillon cubes in boiling water in a saucepan. Combine the curry powder and flour and stir this mixture carefully into the bouillon, stirring constantly to blend. Bring to a boil and add the hot dog mixture. Cover and simmer until hot dogs are heated through, about 10 minutes. Serve with rice.

Serves 4

Quick and Easy Hot Dog Potato Soup

4 hot dogs
4 slices bacon, cut into tiny pieces
1 onion, chopped
1½ cups chicken broth
1 teaspoon celery salt
1 (4 servings) package of instant mashed potatoes
1 (8-ounce) can whole kernel corn
1½ cups milk
Salt and pepper to taste

Cook the bacon and hot dogs cut into ½-inch slices in a heavy saucepan until the bacon is crisp. Remove bacon and reserve. Spoon off all but 2 tablespoons of the fat. Add the onion and cook over low heat until onion is tender. Add the broth and celery salt. Heat to boiling. Remove from heat. Stir the package of instant mashed potatoes and the milk into the soup. Stir in the corn, including its liquid. Heat through. Add salt, pepper and crumbled bacon.

Serves 4 to 6

Chapter 9:

Brands, Cooking, and Eating

Some hot dog aficionados are "hot dog snobs," eating only the private-label brands made and served at hot dog stands and restaurants. Others—and I'm in this camp—heartily enjoy many of the commercial brands you can buy at the supermarket or convenience store.

There are a number of ways to cook hot dogs, each with its pros and cons:

- *Microwave.* Many hot dog aficionados do not approve of microwaved hot dogs, and I used to be one of them. The reason? Juiciness is a key characteristic of a good hot dog, and microwaved dogs tend to "sweat" some of their juice out while cooking; you can see the liquid soak into a paper towel underneath the dog you're nuking.

My youngest son Stephen, on the other hand, enjoys hot dogs cooked in the microwave oven. There's a recipe for microwave hot dogs in chapter 8. In my opinion, microwaving produces a decent dog quickly, but the taste is not comparable to a grilled or broiled dog.

The main reason to microwave, of course, is speed: Put a refrigerated hot dog in the microwave, and you can have a hot, ready-to-eat frankfurter in 60 to 90 seconds—the perfect solution for hungry kids.

- *Grilling.* A favorite of summer backyard barbecues, hot dogs can be grilled over hot coals. The taste is superb, but the downside is that the grilled dogs can get burned or blackened; many kids especially don't like grilling for this reason.

Hot dogs are one of the five most popular grilling meats for barbecue, according to a survey by the National Hot Dog & Sausage Council. Other favorites include sausages, steaks, hamburgers, and chicken.

According to Stephanie Richardson Lawson, a spokesperson for the Barbecue Industry Association, gas grills are acceptable, but "dyed-in-the-wool barbecue fans swear there's no taste like the taste of [meat] cooked on a charcoal grill ... real barbecuing takes place over charcoal briquettes."

The association recently conducted a consumer survey to find out why barbecuing is so popular. The results showed that 82 percent of people who barbecue said it was because they like the flavor, 72 percent said they barbecue because it's easy, and 64 percent said they did it because they enjoy the outdoors.

According to the National Hot Dog & Sausage Council, hot dogs should be kept cool in the refrigerator or an ice-cold cooler until ready to grill. Even though hot dogs are pre-cooked, they should be heated on the grill until steaming hot. Separate hot dogs from other uncooked meats and poultry, and place on a clean plate after grilling.

Observe all hot dog package expiration dates. If you're not sure whether meat or poultry is safe to eat, call the USDA Meat and Poultry Hotline at 1-800-535-4555.

Hot dogs, along with hamburgers, are one of the more portable outdoor cook-out foods: you don't need utensils or even a plate to eat them, so you can carry them almost anywhere. One of my relatives used to take advantage of the dog's portability and eat his frank near the bug zapper to keep the flies away.

But now researchers at Kansas State University say it's a bad idea, because when the bugs are zapped, the device spreads all the bacteria or viruses they were carrying within a 6-foot radius of the machine. You're better off putting the bug zapper in a far corner of the yard and eating your dog at the table with everyone else.

Even if the bugs are biting, never grill your franks indoors. According to Ann Brown, of the Consumer Product Safety Commission, there are 25 deaths a year caused by carbon monoxide poisoning from indoor grilling.

- *Broiling.* Next to grilling on the barbecue, my favorite way to cook a hot dog is in the broiler. Just place them on a piece of aluminum foil and turn once.

- *Boiling.* Hot dogs can be boiled in a pot or simmered in a pan of water. Makes an acceptable dog, but lacks the flavor of broiled or grilled.

- *Steaming.* Put water in the lower chamber of a rice steamer and boil. Place hot dogs in the upper chamber alongside the buns. Remove both when the hot dogs are done and the buns are warm. Like boiled franks, steamed dogs are a bit bland.

- *Deep-frying.* When I was a teenager, I worked as a short-order cook at a snack bar at a town pool. People loved our hot dogs. The secret? We would cook them in the same deep-fryer where we made our French fries. When the hot dogs rose to the surface of the bubbling grease, they were done. Delicious but fattening!

Hot dogs are not naturally a greasy food, but when you deep-fry them, they take on an enormous amount of grease. Best suggestion: roll the deep-fried hot dogs in paper towels to soak up the excess grease.

Also, don't pour the grease down your drain when cooking hot dogs this way at home. Restaurants that fry food often have special grease traps installed in their drain pipes. Environmental Biotech, a Florida company, sells bacteria to restaurants that are meant to be flushed down the drain, where they convert the grease into carbon dioxide and water.

"Yes, Boston has its beans, New Orleans has its gumbo, and Philadelphia has its cheese steaks," writes New Jersey reporter John Cichowski. "But North Jersey holds up its regional end of the menu with deep-fried dogs smothered in spicy brews unavailable almost anywhere else."

At the Rutt Hut in Clifton, the hot dogs are deep-fried in fat that reaches 310 degrees F. "The result is a hot dog that crackles or, as my husband put it, 'a New York hot dog on Viagra,'" says *New York Times* restaurant reviewer Fran Schumer. The Rutt Hut uses the following terminology to describe the various ways they prepare hot dogs:

Ripper—a hot dog whose skin has cracked.
Weller—a well-done ripper.
Medium—moderately well-cooked.

In-and-outer—rare.
Cremator—burned.

"There's a real tradition of the deep-fried dog up north," says John Chirone, proprietor of Hot Dog Johnny's in Buttzville, New Jersey. "The whole Texas Wiener thing centers around the deep-fried dog."

At the Hot Grill in Clifton, New Jersey, the Texas Wiener is blanched in vegetable oil at 350 degrees Fahrenheit. It is then cooked in a pan and served with a chili topping.

- *Hot dog maker. Several companies sell home hot dog makers, a tabletop device specifically designed to cook only hot dogs. The buns and hot dogs are placed in vertical slots, where they are heated like a toaster warms bread. The hot dogs get cooked and the buns get toasted. You can buy this machine from Hammacher Schlemmer (www.hammacher.com; 800-543-3366).*

What Makes a Good Hot Dog?

The answer to the question "What makes a good hot dog?" is naturally subjective. Hot dog lovers almost universally agree, however, that beef and pork dogs are far superior in taste to chicken or turkey dogs.

My informal survey of hot dog lovers showed a preference for kosher over non-kosher franks. As an experiment, I'd ask consumers of non-kosher dogs to try kosher dogs, and usually, once they ate one, they became converted.

Skinless hot dogs, those without casings, are not terribly popular with frank fans either. The cooked casing adds a pleasant crispness that contrasts with the softer meat stuffed inside. "A good hot dog should have a nice snap from a natural casing, a hint of garlic, and a slightly smoky scent," says Jim Bodman, co-chairman, Vienna Beef, Chicago.

"In all top-notch dog houses, the sausage itself is all-beef, long, and fairly slim, dense-textured, with a garlic kick," according to food authors Jane and Michael Stern. "It is steamed until taut enough that a first bite erupts with savory juices on the tongue."

The bun, the Sterns say, should be soft, even "fleecy," serving as a "handy mitt" for the meat within. The basic condiment they recommend: either bright yellow or dark green mustard.

Consumer Reports has set its own standard for what makes a good hot dog:

> Based on taste-tests by trained sensory panelists who measured the intensity of numerous flavor and texture characteristics, an excellent dog should be full-flavored and fairly salty. The hot dog can be a bit sweet and may have onion and garlic flavors. It should also taste fresh, with no old-meat or old-fat flavors. The hot dog should snap with the first bite and be juicy inside. The texture should be slightly springy but not rubbery, and there should be no gritty particles.

The World Famous Hot Dog Page, a Web site devoted to hot dogs (www.xroadsmall.com/tcs/hotdog/best.html), has an online contest where you can vote for the hot dog you think is the best in the world. As of this writing, Nu-Way, with 39 votes, holds the number one position.

Many restaurants nationwide make their own hot dogs rather than serve major brands. Founded in 1916 in Macon, Georgia, Nu-Way is one of the most popular. Nu-Way serves a private-label red weiner (they deliberately misspell it) that is grilled and then stuffed into a steamed bun with mustard, onions, chili sauce, and a mild barbecue sauce containing bits of chopped pork and southern-style coleslaw.

Scot Rodeheaver, who voted for Nu-Way in the contest, says, "Without a doubt, the best hot dogs in the world are found at Nu-Way Wieners. I recently traveled to New York and had a dog from a sidewalk vendor, and it wasn't even close. Nu-Way is the best dog there is."

Another ballot in favor of Nu-Way came from Terry Murphy. He says, "The place is an institution. I grew up in NC and have relatives I would visit every summer in Macon. I could not wait to get down there to get my Nu-Way wiener. Now I have moved to Oregon, and actually have relatives bring them when they come because I miss them so much."

"Anyone visiting Macon or the surrounding area should make a special trip to experience Nu-Way," says Peter D. "Their home-made chili is delicious and they cover the tasty hot dog with slaw, onions, mustard, and anything else you might desire. The buns are toasted to perfection and enhance the taste of this deliciously amazing dog."

In second place, with 18 votes, was Nathan's. One voter comments, "Hands down there is no better than Nathan's. Grilled at their famous stands in New York is the best, although the packaged dogs you find in various parts of the country will do. Complemented with sauerkraut from a big bowl and a little mustard, there's no equal."

Third place, with 16 votes, was Sahlen's, made by Redlinski Meats, which advertises itself as "makers of fine sausage" since 1947.

In fourth place, with 10 votes, was Sabrett. One voter said these dogs were at their best only when served out of a street cart. "The dog has to have been simmering in the water for a minimum of 2 hours, while the roll should be steam-warmed." This is how you get them on street corners in New York City. One New Yorker who also voted for Sabrett said, "Can't beat those dirty water dogs!"

Close behind, with nine votes and in fifth place, was Hebrew National. A Hebrew National fan calls their quarter-pound hot dog "the best, most juicy, delicious, tasty hot dog in the universe."

Beverages to Serve with Hot Dogs

It's really a matter of opinion. Most kids like soda, and most adults like soda, beer, iced tea, or lemonade. Hot dogs are eaten all year long, but since they're often associated with summer—barbecues and cook-outs—they are rarely served with hot beverages.

Milk is not favored by hot dog lovers as an accompanying beverage, although a chocolate milk shake goes good with a dog. This may have its root in the fact that many hot dogs are kosher, and kosher law forbids eating milk and meat together—because, symbolically, it's cruel to boil the calf in the milk of the mother. The Bible tells us not to "boil a kid in its mother's milk." (Ex. 23:19). In addition, there is some evidence that eating meat and dairy together isn't good for your digestion.

I consulted Hugh Johnson's book *How to Enjoy Wine* (Simon and Schuster, 1985), but found no specific recommendations for what wines to drink with a hot dog. In fact, he left me unsure of my previous conviction that red would be the obvious choice over white. "White with fish, red with meat is not a law, like driving on the left when you land at Dover," writes Johnson.

So I posted a query on www.wine.com. The overwhelming first choice from the site visitors was Lemberger, described as "a simple red, with a good deal of fruit." The ideal temperature: slightly chilled.

"If you're going for a red, nothing too heavy or tannic," Tabby advised me. "White wines tend to get smothered by the char grill flavor of barbecued food. A good, fruity red is probably your best bet—a Grenache, for example, or a Merlot. And nothing too expensive … barbecues are for fun drinking."

She continued, "Lemberger is another name for the Hungarian grape, Kekfrankos. I tasted a great one in 1998." She describes Lemberger as "rich cherry chocolate nose and palate, with a cherry-stone finish."

"Lemberger only sounds weird, but it's true *Vitis vinefera*," adds Randy Caparaso. "It's simple—giving straightforward, fruity qualities reminiscent of strawberry or raspberry jam with a twist of black pepper—and generally soft in tannin, and so quite easy to drink and pair with simple foods, from seafood to barbecued meats.

Other wines recommended for pairing with hot dogs by Web site surfers include 1998 Gabrielli Sangiovese Rosato (Redwood Valley), Joseph Phelps Grenache Rose, and Chianti.

Favorite Side Dishes

Potato chips are an overwhelming favorite. There's nothing like sitting in the backyard, grilled hot dog and roll in one hand, the other hand scooping up chips from a bowl.

Others include pickles, potato salad, macaroni salad, coleslaw, French fries, baked beans, and onion rings.

Side dishes that don't go well with hot dogs are baked potatoes, broccoli, mushrooms, peas, and salad.

Hot Dog Manufacturers

Armour Swift-Eckrich
708-512-1612

Ball Park Franks
Hygrade Food Products Corporation
A subsidiary of Sara Lee Corp.
40 Oak Hollow Road #355
Southfield, MI 48034
Phone 810-355-1100

Hebrew National Kosher Foods
A division of Armour Swift-Eckrich
600 Food Center Drive
Bronx, NY 10474
Phone 718-842-5000

Nueske Smoked Wieners
Nueske's Hillcrest Farm
Rural Route 2
PO Box D
Wittenberg, Wisconsin 54499-0904
1-800-392-2266

Nueske Wieners are made from seasoned pork and beef stuffed in natural casings and smoked over glowing embers of Wisconsin apple wood. Each link weighs approximately 2 ounces.

Oscar Mayer Foods
A division of Kraft Foods
910 Mayer Avenue
Madison, WI 53704
Phone 800-222-2323

Sabrett
375 Chestnut Street
Norwood, NJ 07648
Phone 201-935-3330

Thumann Inc.
670 Dell Road
Carlstadt, NJ 07072
Phone 201-935-3636

Shofar Kosher Foods
Bessin Corporation
1001 West Exchange Avenue
Chicago, IL 60609
Phone 773-650-5900

Vienna Beef
2501 N. Damen Ave.
Chicago, IL 60647
Phone 773-278-7800

Select Hot Dogs and Their Ingredients

Nathan's Famous
8 Skinless Franks
Net Wt. 16 oz (1 lb.)

Ingredients: Beef, Water, Salt, Sorbitol, Hydrolyzed Soy, Corn and Wheat Gluten Protein, Paprika, Natural Flavorings, Sodium Erythrobate, Sodium Nitrate

Nutrition Facts
Serving Size 1 Frank (57g)
Servings 8
Calories 160
Fat Cal. 130

	Amount/Serving	%DV*
Total Fat	15g	23%
Sat. Fat	6g	30%
Cholest.	30mg	10%
Sodium	490mg	20%
Total Carb.	1g	0%
Fiber	0g	0%
Sugars	0g	0%
Protein	7g	0%
Vitamin A	–	0%
Vitamin C	–	0%
Calcium	–	0%
Iron	–	4%

*Percent Daily Values (DV) are based on a 2,000 calorie diet.

Hebrew National—Reduced Fat
7 Beef Franks
Net Wt. 12 oz.

Ingredients: Beef, Water, Salt, Hydrolyzed Soy Protein, Flavorings, Paprika, Potassium Chloride, Potassium Phosphates, Garlic Powder, Sodium Erythrobate, Sodium Nitrate

Nutrition Facts
Serving Size 1 Frank (48g)
Servings 7
Calories 120
Fat Cal. 90

	Amount/Serving	%DV*
Total Fat	10g	15%
Sat. Fat	4g	20%
Cholest.	25mg	8%
Sodium	350mg	15%
Total Carb.	1g	0%
Fiber	0g	0%
Sugars	0g	0%
Protein	8g	0%
Vitamin A	–	0%
Vitamin C	–	0%
Calcium	–	0%
Iron	–	4%

*Percent Daily Values (DV) are based on a 2,000 calorie diet.

Oscar Mayer—Big & Juicy Franks
6 Franks
Net Wt. 16 oz. (1 lb.)

Ingredients: Beef, Water, Contains Less Than 2% of Salt, Flavor, Corn Syrup, Dextrose, Sodium Phosphates, Extractives of Paprika, Sodium Erythrobate (made from sugar), Sodium Nitrate

Nutrition Facts
Serving Size 1 Frank (76g)
Servings 6
Calories 240
Fat Cal. 200

	Amount/Serving	%DV*
Total Fat	22g	34%
Sat. Fat	10g	50%
Cholest.	50mg	17%
Sodium	730mg	30%
Total Carb.	1g	0%
Protein	9g	0%
Iron	—	8%

Not a significant source of dietary fiber, sugars, vitamin A, vitamin C and calcium.

*Percent Daily Values (DV) are based on a 2,000 calorie diet.

Sabrett—Skinless Beef Frankfurters
8 Franks
Net Wt. 16 oz (1 lb.) 454g

Ingredients: Beef, Water, Salt, Sorbitol, Flavorings, Paprika, Garlic Powder, Hickory Smoke Flavor, Sodium Erythrobate, Sodium Nitrate

Nutrition Facts
Serving Size 1 Frank (57g)
Servings 8
Calories 170
Fat Cal. 140

	Amount/Serving	%DV*
Total Fat	15g	24%
Sat. Fat	6g	29%
Cholest.	20mg	7%
Sodium	530mg	22%
Total Carb.	1g	0%
Dietary Fiber	0g	0%
Sugars	0g	0%
Protein	7g	0%
Vitamin A	–	0%
Vitamin C	–	0%
Calcium	–	2%
Iron	–	10%

*Percent Daily Values (DV) are based on a 2,000 calorie diet.

Armour Premium Hot Dogs
10 Skinless Franks
Net Wt. 16 oz (1 lb.)

Ingredients: Mechanically Separated Chicken, Water, Meat Ingredients (Pork, Beef), Corn Syrup, Salt, Potato Starch, Contains 2% or Less of Dextrose, Flavorings, Oleoresin of Paprika, Sodium Erythrobate, Sodium Nitrate, Sodium Phosphate, Soy Flour, Sugar

Nutrition Facts
Serving Size 1 Hot Dog (45g)
Servings 10
Calories 120
Fat Cal. 90

	Amount/Serving	%DV*
Total Fat	10g	15%
Sat. Fat	3.5g	18%
Cholest.	30mg	10%
Sodium	450mg	19%
Total Carb.	3g	1%
Fiber	0g	0%
Sugars	1g	0%
Protein	4g	8%
Vitamin A	–	0%
Vitamin C	–	0%
Calcium	–	4%
Iron	–	2%

*Percent Daily Values (DV) are based on a 2,000 calorie diet.

Ball Park Bun Size Franks
8 Franks
Net Wt. 16 oz (1 lb.) 454g

Ingredients: Beef and Pork, Mechanically Separated Chicken, Water, Corn Syrup, Salt, Potassium Lactate, Flavorings, Hydrolyzed Beef Stock, Sodium Phosphate, Ascorbic Acid (Vitamin C), Sodium Nitrate, Extractives of Paprika

Nutrition Facts
Serving Size 1 Frank (56g)
Servings 8
Calories 180
Fat Cal. 150

	Amount/Serving	%DV*
Total Fat	16g	25%
Sat. Fat	6g	29%
Cholest.	40mg	12%
Sodium	620mg	26%
Potassium	420mg	12%
Total Carb.	3g	1%
Fiber	0g	0%
Sugars	2g	0%
Protein	6g	0%
Vitamin A	–	0%
Vitamin C	–	6%
Calcium	–	4%
Iron	–	4%

*Percent Daily Values (DV) are based on a 2,000 calorie diet.

Appendix A:

A Hot Dog Story:

Prince Myshkin and Hold the Relish
by Harlan Ellison

It's not only that Pink's has the best dogs in what we have come to accept as the civilized world (and that includes Nathan's, the original stand out at Coney Island, not those fast-shuffle mickey-mouse surrogates they've opened up from time to time all the way from Broadway to the San Fernando Valley, which, in a less enlightened era, I thought was the dispenser of the *ne plus* ultra of frankfurters), it is also that Michael, who works at Pink's, is one of the best conversationalists on the subject of Dostoevsky in what we have come to accept as the civilized world (and that includes the academic-turned-screenwriter from New York who did a sorta kinda

Dostoevskian film about an academic-turned-gambler, back in 1974).

Which double incentive explains why I was down there at 711 N. La Brea Avenue, almost at the corner of Melrose, at Pink's, founded in 1939 by Paul Pink with a pushcart at that very same location where a heaven-sent hot dog cost a decent 10¢, what now sets one back a hefty dollar-and-a-quarter punch under the heart, even if the quality of dog has not diminished one iota, or even a random scintilla...quality and Michael Bernstein who knows what there is to know about the Fabulous Fyodor were the double incentives to drag me out at dead midnight.

Because I had been lying there in bed, all the way out on the top of the Santa Monica Mountains in the middle of the Mulholland Scenic Corridor, overlooking the twinkling lights of the bedroom communities of the San Fernando Valley which, I have been led to believe, each one represents a broken heart that couldn't make it to Broadway, unable to sleep, tossing and turning, turning and tossing, widdershins and tormented, backing and filling in my lightly starched bedsheets, and of a sudden visions, not of sugar plums, but of dancing hot dogs, fandangoing frankfurters, waltzing wienies, gavotted through my restless head. Eleven-thirty, for God's sake, and all I could think about was sinking my fangs into a Pink's hot dog and discussing a little Karamazov hostility with this Israeli savant who ladles up chili dogs on the graveyard shift behind the steam table. Go figure it. Facts are definitely facts.

So at midnight I'm pulling into the parking spaces beside Pink's, right next door to that shoe store that sells funny Italian disco shoes the heels of which fall off if you spin too quickly in the misguided belief that you are the reincarnation of Valentino or merely just the latest Travoltanoid to turn female heads, and I'm slouching up to the counter, and Michael sees me coming even before I'm out of the car and he's got a hot one working, ready to hand me as I lean up against the clean but battered stainless steel counter.

Just a dog, light on the mustard, hold the relish. No chili, yuchhh the chili; I'm a purist.

And as the front four sink into that strictly kosher nifty, Michael opens with the following: "It wasn't his fault he was so mean to women. Dostoevsky was a man swayed by passions. Two of these, his lamentable love for Paulina Suslova and his obsession for gambling, overlapped."

I'm halfway finished with the first frank as Michael is building the second, and I respond, "You see how you are? You, like everyone else, are ready to condemn a genius simply because he was a liar, a cheat, a pathological gambler who borrowed from his friends and never paid them back, a man who deserted his wife and children, an epileptic existentialist who merely wrote at least half a dozen of the greatest works of fiction the world has ever seen. If he brutalized women it was simply another manifestation of his tormented soul and give me another dog, light on the mustard, hold the relish."

Having now defined the parameters of our evening's discussion, we could settle down to arguing the tiniest, most obscure points; as long as the heartburn didn't start and the hungry hookers and junkies coming in for sustenance didn't distract Michael too much.

"Ha!" Michael shouted, aiming his tongs at my head. "Ha! And Ha again! You fall into the trap of accepted cliché. You mythologize the Russian soul, several thousands years' retroactive angst. When the simple truth that every man in Dostoevsky's novels treats women monstrously invalidates your position. The canon itself says you are wrong!

"Name one exception of substance. Not a minor character, a major one; a moving force, an image, an icon…name one!"

I licked my fingers, nodded for my third sally of the night and said, with the offensive smugness of one who has lured his worthy opponent hip deep into quicksand, "Prince Myshkin."

Michael was shaken. I could tell, shaken: he slathered too much mustard onto the dog. Shaken, he wiped off the excess with a paper napkin and, shaken, he handed it across to me. "Well...yes...of course, Myshkin..." he said slowly, devastated and groping for intellectual balance. "Yes, of course, he treated women decently...but he was an idiot!"

And the six-foot-two pimp with the five working girls at the far end of the counter started screaming about sleazy like honkie muthuhfuckuh countermen who let their Zionist hatred of Third World peoples interfere with the speedy performance of their duties. "But...the image of the brutalizer of women was the one with which Dostoevsky identified..." He started toward the other end of the counter where black fists were pounding on stainless steel.

"Myshkin was the model," I called after him. "Some men are good for women..."

He held up a chili-stained finger for me to hold that place in the discussion, and rushed away to quell the lynch tenor in the mob.

As I stood there, I look across La Brea Avenue. The street was well-lit and I saw this guy standing at the curb right in front of the Federated Stereo outlet, all dressed up around midnight in a vanilla-flavored ice cream suit as pale and wan as the cheek of a paperback heroine, his face ratty and furtive under a spectacular Borsalino hat that cast a shadow across his left eye. Natty and spiffy, but something twitchoid and on the move about him. And as I stood there, waiting for Michael to come back so I could tell him how good some men are for some women, this ashen specter comes off the curb, looking smartly left and right up and down La

Brea, watching for cars but also watching for typhoons, souwesters, siroccos, monsoons, khamsins, Santa Anas and the fall of heavy objects. And as I stood there, he came straight across the avenues and onto the sidewalk there at the front of Pink's, and he slouched to a halt right beside me, and leaned up close with one elbow on the counter touching my sleeve, and he thumbed back the Borsalino so I could see both of his strange dark little eyes, set high in his feral, attractive, strange dark little face, and this is what he said to me:

"Okay. That is it. Now listen up.

"The first girl I ever fell in love with was this raven-tressed little beauty who lived down the block from me when I was in high school in Conshohocken, Pennsylvania. She was sixteen, I was seventeen, and her father opened an apple orchard. Big deal, I said; big fucking deal. An apple orchard. We're not talking here the Sudetenland. Nonetheless, he thought he was landed gentry, my old man worked with his hands over in Kutztown. So we ran away. Got all the way to Eunice, New Mexico, walking, hitching, slipping and sliding, sleeping out in the rain, she comes down with pneumonia and dies at a lying-in hospital over at Carlsbad.

"I'm shook. I'm ruined. What I'm sayin' here, I was distraught.

"Next thing I know I'm signed up with the Merch Marine, shipped out to Kowloon. Twenty minutes in town on shore leave I fall across this Little transistor girl named Orange Blossom. I don't ask questions. Maybe her name was Sun Yung Sing, how'm I to know? She likes me, I like her, we go off hand and hand to make a little rice music. If you catch my drift. Sweet, this was sweet, two young kids, okay so it's miscegenation, a little intermingling of the Occidental with the Oriental, so what? It was purely sweet, and we're talking here about cleaning up some bad leftover feelings. I treat her good, she has respect for an innocent young man, everything's going only terrific until we're walking up

Three Jade Lacquer Box Road looking for this swell little dimsum joint that's been recommended to us, when some nut case off a harbor junk that caught fire and killed his wife and three kids comes running down the street brandishing a kuki, this large knife used for hunting and combat purposes by the Nepalese Gurkhas, and he sticks it right through this sweet little kid possibly named Orange Blossom, and the next thing I know she's lying in a pool of it, right at my feet as this maniac goes screaming up Three Jade Lacquer Box Road.

"Well let me tell you. I'm devastated. Freaked out of my mind. I'm down on my knees wailin' and cryin', what else was there to do?

"So I get myself shipped back home to recuperate, try to blow it all away, try to forget my sorrow, they put me in a VA hospital even though I'm not a vet, they figure, you know, the Merch Marine's as good as the service. Well, I'm not in the hospital three days when I met this terrific candy striper name of Herurietta. Blonde hair, blue eyes, petite little figure, a warm and winning personality.

"She takes a real fancy to me, sees I'm in need of extensive chicken soup therapy, slips in late at night when the ward's quiet and gets under the covers with me. We fall desperately in love, I'm on the mend, we go out to lightweight pizza dinners and G-rated movies. Move in with me, she says, when my time is up at the hospital. Move in with me and we'll whistle a jaunty tune forevermore. Okay, says I, okay you got it. So I move in all my worldly possessions, I'm not there three weeks when she slips boarding a number 10 uptown bus, the doors close on her left foot and she's dragged half a city block before the driver realizes the thumping sound is her head hitting the street.

"So I'm left with the lease on a four-room apartment in San Francisco, you might think that's a neat thing to have, what with the housing shortage, but I'm telling you friend, without love even the Taj Mahal is a cold water flat. So I can't take it, I'm whipped, really downtrodden, sorrowful and in misery.

"I know I shouldn't, but I get involved with this older women on the rebound. She's sixty-one, I'm twenty, and all she can do is do for me. All right, I admit it, this wasn't such straight thinking, but I'm crippled, you know what I mean? I'm a fledging bird with a crippled wing. I need some taking care of, some bringing out of myself. She's good medicine, maybe a little on the wrinkled side but who the hell says a sixty-one-year-old women ain't entitled to a little affection too?

"Everything's going great, strictly great; I move in with her on Nob Hill, we go for long walks, take in Bizet operas, Hungarian goulash in Ghirardelli Square, open and frank discussions about clitoral stimulation and the Panama Canal. All good, all fine, until one night we go a little too deeply into the Kama Sutra and she has this overwhelming uplifted celestial experience which culminates in massive cardiac infarction, so I'm adrift again, all alone on the tides of life, trying to find a soul mate with whom I can traverse the desert of loneliness.

"Then in rapid succession I meet Rosalinda, who gets polio and refuses to see me because she's going to be an invalid the rest of her life; Norma, whose father kills her because she's black and I'm white and he's disappointed she'd rather be just a housewife for some white guy than the world's first black female heart transplant specialist; Charmaine, who was very high on me till she got hit by a cinder-block dropped from a scaffold on a construction job where she was an architect in training, working during her summer college session toward a degree in building stuff; Olive, who was a stewardess who got along fine with me even though our political orientation was very different, until her dinner flight to Tucson came in a little too low and they sent me what was left of her in a very nice imitation Sung dynasty vase from the Federal Aeronautics Administration; and Fernanda and Erwina and Corinne, all of whom wound up in destructive relationships with married men; and finally I meet Theresa, we'll call her Terry, she preferred Terry, I meet her at the track, and we're both on the same horse, a nice little two-year-old name of Leo Rising, and we get to the window at the same time and I ask her what's her sign, because I overhear what horse she's betting, and she says Virgo, and I say I'm a Virgo, and I ask her what's her rising sign and she says, of course Leo, and I say so's mine, and the next thing I know we're dating heavily, and she's gifted me with a sterling silver ID bracelet with my name on the front and With Love From Terry on the reverse, and I've gifted her with a swell couple strands genuine natural simulated pearls, and we name the date, and we post the bands whatever that means, and I meet her family and she can't meet mine because I haven't seen mine in about twenty years, and everything is going just swell when she's out in Beverly Hills going to select her silver pattern, something simple but eloquent in Gorham, and they left a manhole cover off a sewer thing, and she slips and falls and breaks her back in eleven places, her neck and both arms.

"Sweet kid never comes out of the coma, they keep her on the machine nine months, one night her father slips in there on all fours and chews off the plug on the electrical connection, she goes to a much-needed peace.

"So that's it. That's the long and the short of it. Here I am, deeply distressed, not at all settled in my mind, at sixes and sevens, dulled and quite a bit diminished, gloomy, apathetic, awash in tribulation and misery, confused and once more barefoot on the road of life.

"Now what do you think of that?"

And he looks at me.

I look at him.

"Hmmmpf," he snorts. "Try and find a little human compassion."

And he walks off, crosses La Brea at the corner, turns left onto Melrose, and disappears.

I'm still standing there, staring at where he'd been, when Michael comes over, having the pimp and his staff. It had been there minutes; three minutes tops.

"What was that all about?" he asks.

I think I focused on him.

"On the other hand," I say, "there are some guys who are strictly no god dammed good for a women."

Michael nods with satisfaction and hands me a frankfurter. Light on the mustard, pleasantly devoid of the relish.

Bibliography

Books

Favorite Brand Name Recipes. New York: Beekman House, 1981.

More Favorite Brand Name Recipes. New York: Beekman House, 1984.

Good Housekeeping's Hamburger and Hot Dog Cook Book. Chicago: Consolidated Book Publishers, 1958.

Snack and Sandwich Cookbook. New York: Golden Apple Publishers, 1986.

The Fable of the Hot Dog Vendor. Stanislaus Food Products, 1997.

Antol, Marie. *The Incredible Secrets of Mustard.* New York: Avery Publishing Group, 1999.

Asimov, Isaac. *Asimov's Chronology of Science and Discovery.* New York: HarperCollins, 1994.

AvRutick, Fran. *Kosher Cookery.* Middle Village, NY: Jonathan David Publishers, 1989.

Ballantine, Rudolph. *Diet and Nutrition: A Holistic Approach*. Honesdale, PA: Himalayan International Institute, 1978.

Beard, James and Aaron, Sam. *How to Eat Better for Less Money*. New York: Simon & Schuster, 1970.

Biddle, Wayne. *A Field Guide to Germs*. New York: Doubleday, 1995.

Brallier, Jess M. *The Hot Dog Cookbook*. Old Saybrook, CT: The Globe Pequot Press, 1993.

Bridges, Bill. *The Great Chili Book*. New York: Lyons & Burford, 1981.

Coe, Sue. *Dead Meat*. New York: Four Walls Eight Windows, 1995.

Collins, Val. *The Beginner's Guide to Microwave Cookery*. North Pomfret, VT: David & Charles, 1982.

Considine, D.M. and G.D. *Foods and Food Production Encyclopedia*. New York: Van Nostrand Reinhold Company, 1982.

Eisnitz, Gail A. *Slaughterhouse*. Amherst, NY: Prometheus Books, 1997.

Garfunkel, Trudy. *The Kosher Companion*. Secaucus, NJ: Carol Publishing, 1997.

Gelbert, Doug. *So Who the Heck Was Oscar Mayer?* New York: Barricade Books, 1996.

Gordon-Smith, Claire. *Mustard.* Philadelphia: Courage Books, 1998.

Gould, John A. *The Great Little Hot Dog Cook Book.* New York: Doubleday, 1973.

Graulich, David. *The Hot Dog Companion.* Lebhar-Friedman Books, 1999.

Griffin, David. *Any Way You Cut It.* Lawrence, KS: University of Kansas Press, 1995.

Hampton, Sheldon, and Stauber, John. *Mad Cow USA.* Monroe, Maine: Common Courage Press, 1997.

Handwerker, Murray. *Nathan's Famous Hot Dog Cookbook.* New York: Grosset & Dunlap, 1968.

Harland, Marion. *Common Sense in the Household.* New York: Charles Scribner's Sons, 1871.

Hemminger, Jane. *Food Safety: A Guide to What You Really Need to Know.* Ames, Iowa: Iowa State University Press, 2000.

Hogan, David G. *Selling 'em by the Sack.* New York: New York University Press, 1997.

Holland, Barbara. *Endangered Pleasures.* Boston: Little, Brown & Company, 1995.

Johnson, Hugh. *How to Enjoy Wine.* New York: Simon & Schuster, 1985.

Jonas, Howard. *On a Roll.* New York, NY: Viking, 1998.

Jones, Charlotte Foltz. *Mistakes That Worked.* New York: Doubleday, 1991.

Jordan, Michele Anna and Strong, Michael. *The Good Cook's Book of Mustard.* Addison-Wesley, 1994.

Kaufman, William I. *The Hot Dog Cook Book.* New York: Doubleday, 1966.

Kaufmann, Klaus and Schoneck, Annelis. *The Cultured Cabbage.* BC Canada: Alive Books, 1997.

Kiple, Kenneth and Ornelas, Kriemnild, Editors, *The Cambridge World History of Food.* Cambridge: Cambridge University Press, 2000.

Lauber, Patricia. *Tales Mummies Tell.* New York: HarperCollins, 1985.

Lee, Laura. *The Name's Familiar.* Gretna, Louisiana: Pelican Publishing, 1999.

Marcus, Erik. *Vegan: The New Ethics of Eating.* Ithaca, NY: McBooks Press, 1998.

Merinoff, Linda. *The Savory Sausage.* New York, NY: Poseidon Press, 1987.

Mettler, John J. Jr. *Basic Butchering of Livestock and Game.* Pownal, Vermont: Storey Communications, Inc., 1986.

Miller, Gustav Hindman. *10,000 Dreams Interpreted.* Dorset, England: Element Books, 1996.

Naj, Amal. *Peppers: A Story of Hot Pursuits.* New York: Vintage Books, 1992.

Predika, Jerry. *The Sausage-Making Cookbook.* Mechanicsburg, PA: Stackpole Books, 1983.

Rampton, Sheldon and Stauber, John. *Mad Cow U.S.A.* Monroe, Maine: Common Courage Press, 1997.

Reavis, Charles G. *Home Sausage Making.* Pownal, VT: Storey Communications, 1987.

Roate, Mettja C. *The New Hamburger and Hot Dog Cook Book.* New York: WeatherVane Books, 1975.

Ryback, David. *Look 10 Years Younger, Live 10 Years Longer.* Englewood Cliffs, NJ: Prentice Hall, 1995.

Saltzberg, Barney. *This Is a Great Place for a Hot Dog Stand.* New York: Hyperion Books, 1995.

Schlosser, Eric. *Fast Food Nation.* Boston: Houghton Mifflin, 2001.

Sebrank, J.G.; Beermann, D.H.; and Axe, J.B. *Meat Science and Food Processing.* Lake Geneva, WI: Peerage Press, 1989.

Sinclair, Upton. *The Jungle.* New York: Bantam, 1981.

Sinatra, Stephen. *Heartbreak and Heart Disease*. New Canaan, CT: Keats, 1996.

Smith, Andrew F. *Pure Ketchup*. Columbia, S.C.: University of South Carolina Press, 1996.

Smith, Herman. *Kitchens Near and Far*. New York: M. Barrows & Co., Inc., 1946.

Spinrad, Leonard and Thelma. *Speaker's Lifetime Library*. West Nyack, NY: Parker Publishing Company, 1979.

Steer, Gina. *Burgers and Hot Dogs*. Edison, NJ: Chartwell Books, 1995.

Stull, Donald; Broadway, Michael; and Griffith, David. *Any Way You Cut It: Meat Processing and Small-Town America*. Lawrence, KS: University of Kansas Press, 1995.

Thompson, Pat. *I Love Hot Dogs*. Port Ludlow, WA: Still News Press, 1982.

Timm, Uwe. *The Invention of Curried Sausage*. New York: New Directions, 1993.

Vitale, Joe. *The Power of Outrageous Marketing*. Niles, IL: Nightingale Conant, 1999. Audio cassette program.

Walsh, David. *The Vidalia Sweet Onion Cookbook*. Memphis, TN: Starr-Toof, 1996.

Winter, Ruth. *A Consumer's Dictionary of Food Additives*. New York: Crown Trade Paperbacks, 1994.

Wolczuk, Alice. *Discovering Sauerkraut*. B.C., Canada: The Caitlin Press (no copyright date).

Yaverbaum, Eric. *Public Relations Kit for Dummies*. Foster City, CA: IDG, 2000.

Periodicals

"A Frank Comparison." *Good Housekeeping* (June 1995): 120.

"A Side of History." *The Sunday Record* (August 10, 1997): T-3.

"Bacteria Take on Grease Traps." *Popular Mechanics* (October 2002): 22.

"Battling Bacteria with Copper." *The Futurist* (October 1998): 2.

"Big Lottery Winner Comes Forward." The Associated Press (May 12, 2000).

"Bill Johnson of Heinz." *Sky* (November 2000): 58-59.

"Darwin Awards." *The Successful Practice* (March 19, 1999): 7.

"Eating Near Bug Zappers Can Be a Hazard." *Record* (June 4, 1999).

"Healthy News." *Health* (September, 2000): 30.

"Hot Dogs: Can They Fit in a Healthful Cookout?" *Consumer Reports* (July, 1993): 418.

"If You Can't Take the Heat." *American Demographics* (May 2000): 72.

"Hot Diggity." *Daily News* (July 9, 1997).

"Hot Dogs." *Consumer Reports* (July, 1993): 415-419.

"Kashrut: Jewish Dietary Laws." The Jewish Student Online Research Center Web site. www.us-israel.org/jsource.html.

"Kicking It Up." *Reader's Digest* (October, 2002): 22.

"Leaner Wieners." *Men's Health* (June 1997): 42.

"Meat Packaging Is an Important Issue for Many Consumers." *Research Alert* (September 7, 2001): 8.

"National Foods." Corporate Background press release.

"One Dog, Holds the Ads." *Sports Illustrated* (January 22, 1990): 9.

"Quick Bite." *New York Times* (May 24, 1998): NJ-7.

"Sara Lee to Pay $4.4 Million to End Tainted Meat Lawsuits." *Record* (June 23, 2001): A12.

"Sausage Links." *Daily News* (March 9, 1998).

"The Bronx That Was." *Daily News* (June 10, 1998): CN-44.

"Top Hot Dog Eater Stuns Competitors." *Record* (July 5, 2001): A4.

"Want to Know More." *New York Times* (May 24, 1998): 8.

"When Only a Wiener Will Do." *Fortune* (October 14, 1996): 28.

"Why Good Sausages Go Bad." *Scientific American* (December, 2000): 14.

Aberback, Brian. "Tastes Great!" *Record* (July 28, 1997): –.

Block, Pamela, "Headshots to Go." *Back Stage West* (October 30, 2002): 4.

Bovsun, Mara. "Farklempt." *Daily News* (March 10, 1998): 23.

Brown, David Jay and Novick, Rebecca McClen, "Nature of the Beast." *The Sun* (October 1998): 7.

Brasher, Philip. "Food Trade Ranging Far Afield in Fighting Dangerous Bacteria." *Record* (June 26, 2001): A12.

Cichowski, John. "Jersey Dogs: A Love Story." *Record* (April 22, 2000) A1.

Di Ionno, Mark. "Let's Be Frank." *Star Ledger* (July 30, 1998): 53.

Fenner, Austin. "Hot Dog! U.S. Eyes Chompionship." *Daily News* (July 3, 1998).

Forgang, Isabel. "Where Culprits Lurk." *Daily News* (June 22, 1998): 33.

Harkins, Deborah. "All Fired Up." *Daily News* (June 4, 1999): CN4.

Gelles, Jeff. "Feds Moving Closer to Approving Irradiated Meat." (April 26, 1999): H-6.

Gethard, Chris, "Stalking the Weird NJ Hot Dog." *Weird NJ* (Issue #17): 51-53.

Gonzalez, Juan. "Mayor Bully's a Hot Dog." *Daily News* (June 2, 1998): 16.

Gordon, Sandra. "Is It Safe to Eat Meat?" *New Age* (December 2001): 40.

Harris, Jeff. "Shortcuts: A Complete Wrap of the Hot Dog." NEA, June 25. Year unknown.

Hinckley, David. "It's Good Again Like Nedick's." *Daily News* (January 14, 2003): 15.

James, George. "An Empire Built on Hot Dogs." *New York Times* (May 24, 1998): 4NJ.

Kannapell, Andrea. "Taking the Wiener to the World." *New York Times* (May 24, 1998): NJ-7.

Kannapell, Andrea. "Or Would You Rather Watch Laws Being Made?" *New York Times* (May 24, 1998): NJ-6.

Keller, Susan Jo. "Good Time, Good Cause." *New York Times* (May 24, 1998): 6NJ.

Kilman, Scott. "Hot Dog Recall Poses Problem for Meat Industry." *Wall Street Journal* (March 31, 2000): 7A.

Lee, Bob. "Japanese Cut Mustard." *Daily News* (July 5, 2000): 5.

Lieber, Ronald. "When Only a Wiener Will Do." *Fortune* (October 14, 1996): 28.

Maeder, Jay. "Nathan Handwerker." *Daily News* (March 31, 1999): 23.

Magelonsky, Marcia. "Home Meal Replacement." *American Demographics* (July 1998): 38.

Mansnerus, Laura. "Homers and Hot Dogs." *New York Times* (May 24, 1998): 7NJ.

Martin, Nina. "New Dogs on the Block." *Health* (April 1992): 20.

McCord, Holly. "Nutrition News." *Prevention* (July 1994): 49.

Oetzel, Donna. "A Consuming Passion." *Restaurants USA* (May, 1998): 22.

Page, Jeffrey. "At the Hot Grill in Clifton." *Record* (October 8, 1999): 26.

Raloff, Janet. "Well-Done Research." *Science News* (April 24, 1999): 264-266.

Rogers. David. "Meat and Poultry Packers Defeat Move to Allow Civil Penalties in the Industry." *Wall Street Journal* (June 17, 1998): A4.

Ross, Emma. "Preserved Red Meat Linked to Cancer." *Record* (June 23, 2001): A12.

Schuman, Patti. "Grilling and Cancer Risk." *Nutrition News* (October, 1996).

Schumer, Fran. "Two Rippers, P.C., With Relish Mother Made." *New York Times* (May 24, 1998): 11 NJ.

Skenazy, Lenore. "Salami's Quest is No Baloney." *Daily News* (November 4, 1997).

Stern, Jane and Michael. "Snack Snacks." *Sky* (July 1999): 52-57.

Stix, Gary. "Homo Carnivorous." *Scientific American* (June 2004): 26.

Strunsky, Steve. "Eating His Way to the Top." *New York Times* (May 24, 1998): 6 NJ.

Taylor, Michael and Hoffmann, Sandra. "Redesigning Food Safety." *Issues in Science and Technology* (Summer 2001): 28.

Tully, Tracey. "Illness Spurs Hot Dog Recall by Feds." *Daily News* (October 14, 1999).

Wild, Russell. "Great Waist Land." *New York Post* (May 15, 2001): 51.

Williams, Florence. "Shtetlers." *The New Republic* (May 19, 1977).

Yellin, Deena. "NJ Pals Trace America's Passion for the Footlong." *Record* (May 2, 1999): A-16.

Web sites

A1. http://www.a1mall.com

Black & Decker. www.blackanddecker.com

Barricks. http://www.barricksinsurance.com

Cecilia Svensson. http://www4.torget.se/users/e/ELViSiss/FOOD/FRANK.HTM

Colman's Mustard. http://www.colmansmustard.com

Itsy's Kitchen. http://mysite.verizon.net/vzeplsuh/kitchen/hotdogs.html

Epicurious dictionary. http://www.epicurious.com

Foot-Long: The Movie. http://www.foot-long.com

Kraft. http://www.kraftfoods.com

Meals for You. http://www.mealsforyou.com

National Hot Dog Month. http://www.flavorweb.com/hotdogmonth.htm

National Hot Dog & Sausage Council. http://www.hotdog.org/

New York City Press Office. http://www.ci.nyc.us/html

Oscar Mayer. http://www.oscar-mayer.com

Sean Wenzel. http://recipes.wenzel.net

Shea Communications. http://www.sheacommunications.com/
frnath.htm

Shona Ward. http://ccnga.uwaterloo.ca

SOAR Searchable Archive of Recipes. http://soar.berkeley.edu/
recipes/hints

Soyfoods Symposium. http://soyfoods.com

The World Famous Hot Dog Page. http://www.xroadsmall.com/
tcs/hotdog/best.html

About the Author

Bob Bly is the author of 100 articles and 70 books including *101 Ways to Make Every Second Count* (Career Press), *Comic Book Heroes* (Carol Publishing), and *The "I Hate Kathie Lee Gifford" Book* (Kensington).

Bob's articles have appeared in such publications as *Cosmopolitan, Amtrak Express, New Jersey Monthly, Science Books & Films, Computer Decisions,* and *Chemical Engineering.* He has lectured before numerous groups including the Mail Order Nursery Association, International Tile Exposition, American Chemical Society, and International Association of Laboratory Distributors. Bob has been a guest on dozens of TV and radio shows, and has appeared on CNBC and CBS's *Hard Copy.*

Bob Bly holds a B.S. in chemical engineering from the University of Rochester and is a member of the American Institute of Chemical Engineers. He loves hot dogs and eats them frequently, despite his high cholesterol.

Questions and comments on *All-American Frank* may be sent to:

Bob Bly
22 E. Quackenbush Avenue
Dumont, NJ 07628
phone 201-385-1220
fax 201-385-1138
e-mail: rwbly@bly.com
Web site: www.bly.com

Printed in the United Kingdom
by Lightning Source UK Ltd.
126237UK00001B/170/A